Teaching in the Age
of Disinformation

Teaching in the Age of Disinformation

Don't Confuse Me with the Data, My Mind Is Made Up!

Selma Wassermann

ROWMAN & LITTLEFIELD
Lanham • Boulder • New York • London

Published by Rowman & Littlefield
A wholly owned subsidiary of The Rowman & Littlefield Publishing Group, Inc.
4501 Forbes Boulevard, Suite 200, Lanham, Maryland 20706
www.rowman.com

Unit A, Whitacre Mews, 26–34 Stannary Street, London SE11 4AB

British Library Cataloguing in Publication Information Available

Library of Congress Cataloging-in-Publication Data Is Available
ISBN 978-1-4758-4097-1 (cloth: alk. paper)
ISBN 978-1-4758-4098-8 (pbk: alk. paper)
ISBN 978-1-4758-4099-5 (electronic)

♾™ The paper used in this publication meets the minimum requirements of American National Standard for Information Sciences—Permanence of Paper for Printed Library Materials, ANSI/NISO Z39.48–1992.

Printed in the United States of America

Contents

Preface

An elementary school teacher with many years of classroom experience was being interviewed at my university for a position as a faculty associate, responsible for the supervision of student teachers. One of the questions posed to him by one of the members of the selection committee at the end of his ordeal was: What do you consider to be the most important task in your work with students preparing to become teachers?

Sol had no trouble responding. "I would want them to know 'what's important' in preparing their students to teach."

This is a question that I have reflected on since I heard it raised—and, of course, have come to understand that "what's important" is more often influenced by current situations, as well as with teachers' views of what they see as their most important teaching and learning goals. For example, during the harsh and bitter days of World War II, what was important in classrooms across the country was overt and palpable support for the war effort and for the men in battle—and those goals took a front seat in the what and the how of classroom practice.

In the peace that followed the unconditional surrender of the Axis forces, what was important was teaching reading, writing, numbering, and spelling—a "getting back to the basics." A few years later, when the Russians launched Sputnik, what rose to the top of the list was science—teaching and encouraging students to become more knowledgeable, more interested, and more creative in the various scientific fields that would put the country ahead in its scientific endeavors.

When President George W. Bush took office, his alarm over the lapses in children's reading and writing abilities led to his advancement of "No Child Left Behind"—an administrative initiative to promote literacy skills. In a perverse understanding of "what was important," performance on standardized literacy tests took precedence over other subjects, such as science and social studies. Music and art got short shrift.

What's important in education is influenced to a large extent by what is happening in our culture and by what is considered by policy makers as those significant learning goals deemed essential to ensure the intellectual health and economic stability of the country.

The "Information Age" has brought a new sense of "what's important" in educational practice. With the onset of the twenty-first century came the miracles and hazards of the 24/7 outpouring of information from sources that, fifty years ago, would have seemed like something out of a Flash Gordon cartoon. Children who are now, arguably, more tech wise than some of their parents spend more time on their computers than they do out of doors. They are at the receiving end of what comes through the ethers, on their tablets, on their smartphones, and on Twitter and social media—the information and the disinformation that shape their thinking, their values, and their decisions. What skills do they have that allow them to differentiate between what is true and what is false? Between what is fact and what is truthiness? Between what is real and what is spin?

Without such ability to discriminate between what is true and what is fantasy, how will such confusion distort their thinking and their decisions? How will they be able to choose wisely if the information on which their choice is based is specious?

In this Information Age, educators are faced with a new mission of "what's important"—that of preparing students at all educational levels to become more wary, more careful, and more intelligent consumers of information—so that they may make better choices, better arguments, and better and wiser ways of dealing with the many issues they will face as adults. As some pundits have already noted, our very democracy may depend on it. Bill Cliett, the former superintendent of schools of Gainesville, has noted, "The ability to use thinking skills to analyze and evaluate the minefield of disinformation we all must navigate today is critical to the fate of our planet and our own survival."

In the many years of my life teaching teachers, this I know with certainty: teachers want very much to make a difference in the lives of their students. They want their work to count for something. It is their sincerest wish that their students become wiser, more informed, more intelligent, more discerning, and more kind to each other. And they are committed to a professional journey, seeking for better methods to bring about those ambitions.

So it is for those teachers and for all who enter the profession that I offer this text. I hope it provides not only the supporting principles that are at the heart of how to reach such noble goals, but also the how to—with numerous suggestions for those teaching practices that bring such goals to realization.

Acknowledgments

This book is dedicated to my great teachers, who patiently, and with great wisdom, opened my mind and enabled me to begin my professional work to make a difference in the lives of my students: Louis E. Raths, Sylvia Ashton-Warner, "Chris" Christensen—to all of whom I owe a debt that can never be adequately repaid.

I also want to thank my group of reviewers, whose insightful and additive comments made a considerable difference in shaping this work: James Raths, Bill Cliett, Judy Feder, and Larry Cuban. I am deeply grateful to you all.

And it is also dedicated to my family members who have always stood with me, supporting and encouraging me in my life's work, with love, humor, and wisdom: Jack, Paula, my beloved grandsons, Arlo and Simon, and, of course, my three adorables, Maya, Kai, and Ruben Maslow.

Introduction

To paraphrase Charles Dickens, "We live in the best of times, we live in the worst of times." Our twenty-first century has seen much progress in many fields of endeavor—medicine, agriculture, ecology, physics, biology, and communication—to name only a few. But with progress came unanticipated downsides and more ethical questions than we had imagined.

When the internet came into being, we were gifted with immediate access to information from myriad sources. No one imagined such a boon would also become a source of misinformation, intimidation, infiltration, and scamming, leaving a huge swath of "users" unable and unready to differentiate between what offers were valid and which were devious ploys to extract money from our bank accounts, between what were facts supported by data and what were blatant lies, and between truths and "alternate truths."

Now, from these many varied sources, we are inundated with information and separating out truth from disinformation has become a skill requiring increasing aptitude, cognitive awareness, suspension of judgment, and critical reasoning. It fact, it would not be an exaggeration to say that there are those in the Ethernet world whose primary goal is to spread such disinformation—for their own nefarious purposes.

For example, one of the singular features of the 2016 presidential election was the extent and nature of disinformation that was intended to manipulate voters' choices. On phone-in talk radio, TV, and the internet, one could hear, for example, that President Obama was a secret Muslim, that Mrs. Clinton ran a child sex ring out of a pizza parlor, that Mr. Obama had a secret plot to subvert Christendom, and that Mrs. Clinton had a string of murder victims to her credit, to name only a few such blatant falsehoods. Even more astonishing was the number of voters who actually believed these infamous lies.

But this kind of disinformation was not just seen in the year 2016. Nor was it limited to the election. Fantastic claims are found in other venues as well, and they give rise to such notions as UFO sightings, landings and abductions by aliens, government cover-ups of nefarious plots, secret alliances with interplanetary beings, vaccinations that cause autism, and contrails composed of exotic chemicals that are part of a secret government scheme to test weapons. Added to such fantasies are beliefs that extraterrestrials built the pyramids, and that the media or the government adds secret mind-controlling technology to television broadcast signals. These beliefs come from various "information" channels and infiltrate the most vulnerable minds to create myths that not only endure but also are resistant to hard data.

The internet and the World Wide Web is a source of much that is positive in our lives, but it also makes it possible for disinformation to be more widely disseminated and thereby more widespread. According to Anderson (2017), "Before the Internet, crackpots were mostly isolated and surely had a harder time remaining convinced of their alternate realities. Now their devoutly believed opinions are all over the airwaves and the web, just like actual news. Now all of the fantasies look real."

If this sounds bizarre, the latest news about the hacking of the internet by "Sputnik," a Russian government–run news and commentary site, cites evidence that in a new information war that Russia is waging against the West, conspiracy theories and outright falsehoods with tenuous connection to fact are amplified until they break through into domestic policies, promoting views that put pressure on the politics of Western governments (Rutenberg 2017).

"Reason remains free to combat unreason, but the Internet entitles and equips all the proponents of unreason and error to a previously unimaginable degree" (Anderson 2017). "What people find on the web creates a whole new permission structure, a sense of social affirmation for what was once unthinkable" (Bruni 2017).

To most rational thinkers, the kind of disinformation that comes cascading down from various media sources would easily be put out to pasture with a smirk and perhaps a grimace. It would be easy to see that such alternate truths were too blatant, too ridiculous, and too unimaginable to be believed. But sad to say, wild theories not only abound, but are also influential factors in decision-making situations. It gives one pause to consider how it is possible that adults, given the public education that is their guarantee in many countries, could embrace such falsehoods with so much passion and obsessive commitment to those particular beliefs. People who are "reality based" are a minority—maybe a third of us, but almost certainly fewer than half (Anderson 2017).

For those of us concerned with the education of children, these are power-ful and harsh realities since youth may be particularly vulnerable to the fake news and conspiracy theories that come at them in large doses via social media. The situation has become so critical that the Italian Ministry of Educa-tion has put into operation a plan to include "training a generation of students steeped in social media how to recognize fake news and conspiracy theories online," since, as the president of the lower house of the Italian Parliament claimed, "Fake news drips drops of poison into our daily web diet and we end up infected without even realizing it" (Horowitz 2017).

Daniel Kahneman (2011), in his book *Thinking Fast and Slow*, wrote about human irrationality—the kind of thinking that distorts our judgment of the world, "our tendency to be influenced by irrelevant numbers that we happen to be exposed to, our flawed human reasoning." He identified two systems that drive the way we think and make choices. System One is fast, intuitive, and emotional. It is easy and doesn't take a lot of mental work. System Two is slower, more deliberative, and more logical. It is harder and requires more mental effort.

Kahneman's work may explain, in part, why it is so easy for some adults to fall into the trap of believing what they read in supermarket tabloids, hear on TV commercials, and accept uncritically what they see on internet sites. It may also explain why the appeal to emotion is so easily manipulated and how difficult it is to overcome emotion with reason.

Hard as it is to believe, a study done at the Sanford Graduate School of Education found "a dismaying inability of students to reason about informa-tion they see on the Internet. For example, students had a hard time distin-guishing advertisements from news articles or identifying where information came from" (Friedman 2017).

"Over the past 18 months, we administered assessments that tap young people's ability to judge online information. We analyzed over 7,804 responses from students in middle school through college. At every level, we were taken aback by students' lack of preparation: middle school students unable to tell the difference between an advertisement and a news story; high school students taking at face value a cooked-up chart from the Min-nesota Gun Owners Political Action Committee; college students credulously accepting a .org top-level domain name as if it were a Good Housekeeping seal" (Wineberg and McGraw 2016).

Hence, "don't confuse me with the data; my mind is made up." Or, alter-natively, "we have countless ways in which we fool ourselves into making bad decisions." And while there is no question that such is the nature of how some people arrive at decisions today, a more important question is: What are the implications for education in our "alternate-truth" era?

If these data have relevance for teachers, administrators, and policy makers, it may be long past time that the educational establishment rethink what education is for and ask: What is being done in classrooms that ignores such "thinking malfunctions" in students? And what is being done in classrooms to combat it and give students many and frequent opportunities to practice and develop more rational habits of mind? To become more discerning interpreters of data? To be more equipped to differentiate between fact and fantasy? To rely more on rational thinking and the suspension of judgment in interpreting data and making decisions of consequence?

As Friedman (2017) has written, "Work on that compact has to start with every school teaching children digital civics. And that begins with teaching them that the Internet is an open sewer of untreated, unfiltered information, where they need to bring skepticism and critical thinking to everything they read and basic civic decency to everything they write."

There are good reasons that teachers are unable to address every problem that students bring to school, every obstacle that gets in the way of their learning, and every demand that is made on their time and their energies. No, teachers cannot fix what is utterly and unhappily broken in students' lives. But surely teachers can give more time to elevate more intelligent habits of mind, to carry out programs that tap into students' rational and reasonable ways of solving problems and making decisions? Surely, teachers can place "teaching for thinking" at the very top of the list of what can and should be done in classrooms at all educational levels—from the very early childhood years to the last days of graduate school.

Surely teachers at every educational level can appreciate not only the importance of this kind of emphasis, but also its absolute urgency. It is with these issues that this book is concerned.

HOW THE BOOK IS ORGANIZED

The book is organized into three sections—each of which provides teachers with the principles, tools, and teaching strategies to enable them to help students develop more intelligent habits of mind.

The three chapters in the first section offer suggestions for what teachers can do, within the constraints of their grade-level curriculum demands, to elevate students' more rational habits of mind. A framework is also suggested for how curriculum may be organized to emphasize teaching for thinking.

In the second section of the book, hundreds of ideas are included for developing curriculum tasks, rooted in the mental operations that call for higher-order thinking, at all grade levels, in virtually all the curriculum areas.

The last section presents teaching strategies that address students' deeply held beliefs that appear resistant to logical examination, how teachers may conduct classroom discussions that promote more thoughtful examination of important issues, using higher-order questions and reflective responses, as well as suggesting methods to assess students' growth.

For teachers who believe in the importance of elevating students' intelligent habits of mind, this book should provide not only the principles but also many research-based tools for classroom work.

Section I

Chapter 1

What Can Teachers Do?

Anyone who has spent any time as a teacher is not a stranger to the kinds of in-school pressures and top-down policies that burden teachers and keep them from doing the best they can do for each and every student in their classrooms. Anyone who has spent any time as a teacher will be familiar with the feelings of frustration that teachers endure at the end of each school day, reflecting on what might have been done for this and that youngster, IF ONLY there were more time or more resources to accomplish that task.

Teachers know too well the problems that many children live with and bring to school, that, despite their best efforts, cannot be "fixed" so that those children can be more ready to learn. Yet, despite all of that, many teachers have found ways to improve students' intelligent habits of mind, giving them more opportunities to become more rational in the way they think and reason. To become, in Kahneman's (2011) words, more "System Two thinkers in their decision making and problem solving."

Learning to do this is not beyond the skills and understanding of teachers. It does not require adding a new course in "thinking" to the curriculum. Instead, it begins with the basic premise of "shifting gears in the curriculum" so that the emphasis is on "thinking" rather than on the more routine tasks of finding answers to questions that are largely irrelevant to what is important, to what really matters.

Such shifting of the "gears" in organizing what is taught is primarily a matter of teachers deciding on "what's important" as they work to deliver the subject matter that is standard and required for each of the elementary and secondary grades. This is not to suggest that these "gear shifts" in the way the curriculum is organized and delivered will turn frogs into princes; but given the data on other long-term work with "teaching for thinking" in classrooms at all levels, it is safe to say that such an approach can make a significant difference to the development of students' intelligent habits of mind (Raths et al. 1986).

There are, however, some caveats to be raised. First, such an approach cannot be relegated to a brief encounter—an add-on in a spare period when nothing else is on schedule—but must become an integral part of what teachers and students do every day, within the major subjects of the curriculum. Second, such a program must be enduring, because teachers cannot expect positive results in a week or even a month. Improvement in habits of intelligent thinking, like learning other life skills, comes with extended experience, practice, and reflection on practice over time.

The data from classroom research studies conducted over many years and at many levels of instruction suggest that four to six months would be the minimum time to expect to see visible signs of positive results (Raths et al. 1986).

And, finally, the bottom line is that only teachers who consider such goals important will commit themselves to such an undertaking.

Chapter 2

Shifting Gears in the Curriculum to Emphasize Teaching for Thinking: An Overview

Most teachers, administrators, and policy makers, as well as many parents, would affirm, in their goals for education, the need for students to develop their abilities to act thoughtfully and maturely, as well as to take on the complex problems of life in the rapidly changing ethos of our twenty-first century. Many teachers, in fact, consider the promotion of students' capacity to be rational consumers of what is read, heard, and seen, a top priority educational goal, perhaps more important today than ever before in the history of education.

Yet, despite the rhetoric, classroom materials in widespread use still emphasize the acquisition of low-level cognitive skills. In terms of materials that are the staple of the instructional diet, school districts still keep buying, and teachers continue to be forced to use texts and workbooks that give pupils extensive practice in the development of lower-order skills. Federal mandates in the United States, like No Child Left Behind and the more recent Common Core Curriculum Standards, have put additional pressure on teachers and students to "teach to the test"—where single correct answers are more important than the quality of thinking that lies behind them.

In short, there is a virtual dearth of instructional materials that require students to practice and gain skill in higher-order cognitive functioning. And too often, administrative directives to use these standard texts preclude teachers' use of materials that encourage student thinking. Because of this subtle and overt institution press, instructional strategies place heavy emphasis on the dissemination of information, where teachers do most of the talking, with students the passive recipients of "knowledge."

These are some of the more obvious conditions that explain why teaching for thinking has not been making significant headway in classroom practice—despite educators' claims that such goals are what education should aspire to. Moving teaching for thinking from our rhetoric into the life of the classroom may require not only a reconceptualization of what we do, but also the understanding of and commitment to where our teaching emphases must lie. In that sense, understanding of how to shift gears—toward those teaching strategies that underlie teaching for thinking—provides not only a paradigm, but also some specific teaching strategies.

This is not to suggest that recalling information and knowing "right" answers are not important. Teachers will, of course, wish to ensure that students know how to add, multiply, and divide, as well as the correct spellings of words—despite the fact that these rudimentary skills are easily accessed by a desktop computer, a tablet, or a smartphone. Teaching for thinking does not mean abandoning the acquisition of information. It means, rather, shifting the emphasis in the curriculum so that information is gathered through a teaching for thinking framework. Inert information is largely useless; it is more the way we use, discern, and interpret information that is key to more informed, intelligent behavior.

A TEACHING FOR THINKING CURRICULUM FRAMEWORK

In 1966, Louis E. Raths (1966) formulated a theory of thinking that was based, largely, on his work with classroom teachers. His theory offered practical help for teachers who were seeking ways to develop students' higher-order cognitive skills.

For example, Raths suggested that students who engaged consistently and frequently in curriculum tasks that called for the higher-order mental functions of comparing, observing, suggesting hypotheses, summarizing, classifying, creating and inventing, searching out assumptions, interpreting data, making decisions and examining consequences, criticizing and evaluating, and designing projects and investigations would not only benefit in their thinking skills, but would also show significant and observable change in behavior associated with poor-quality thinking (Raths et al. 1966, 1–30).

The theory led to many research investigations, at all levels of educational practice, from the primary grades through graduate work at the university level (e.g., Raths et al. 1986, 222–23), all of which supported the theory. In short, it was found that teachers, from the primary grades through graduate school, who engaged their students in curriculum activities that were based in these "thinking operations" would find students showing significant and observable changes in their "thinking-related" behaviors; that is, they become more thoughtful, more circumspect, less likely to make assumptions based on poor evidence, and more able to suspend judgment in determining truth.

Developing curriculum tasks that are rooted in these thinking operations would mean that teachers use the standard curriculum guides as a basis so that students gather the required information by comparing, observing, examining assumptions, interpreting data, making decisions, criticizing and evaluating, summarizing, classifying, suggesting hypotheses, and designing projects and investigations. Curriculum tasks based in these thinking operations could be developed in any subject area and at any grade level.

The thinking operations that require students to "put their minds to work" are more than useful guides in the development of classroom materials that require students to use data in more constructive and mentally active ways. The operations, it will be seen, require students to "do something more" with information—something more than merely absorbing it from a page and recalling facts. This "more" involves more sophisticated and intelligent examination of that information and the suspension of judgment when the data are suspect or unavailable. And that kind of analysis leads to increased understanding of the significant concepts, the "big ideas" in the curriculum.

Using these thinking operations to develop curriculum activities within the subject areas can be an integral part of every subject, that is, teaching subject matter with an emphasis on thinking. So "teaching for thinking" is not a subject; it is a way the subjects are taught. And given the kind and quality of disinformation that lards the media, it would seem of vital importance to use a teaching for thinking framework to examine social issues and to teach students to "prize the doubt."

In chapters 4 through 14, these operations are described in detail and extensive lists of suggestions are offered for the kinds of curriculum activities that could be derived from them, across different subject areas and grade levels.

TO KNOW, TO UNDERSTAND, AND TO KNOW HOW: KEY STEPS IN TEACHING FOR THINKING

The words "to know" are much stressed in educational practice, and much classroom effort is directed toward that goal. All teachers want their students *to know*: the correct spelling, the correct answers to test questions, the names of the fifty states, and the dates of important world events.

But *to know*—the mere gathering of information—does not necessarily mean to understand. A student can know the names of the letters of the alphabet, but not understand how sounds are blended together to form words. A student may know the mechanics of dividing fractions, but not understand about reciprocals. Students may know the mnemonic HOMES to remember the initial consonants of the names of the five Great Lakes, but have no idea of what a "great lake" is, or where the lakes are located, or what their social-economic, political, or geographical importance is. Students may know that Columbus sailed across the Atlantic Ocean in 1492 and the names of his ships, but have no deeper understanding of the meaning of that voyage and its implications for the larger issues surrounding the "discovery" of the continent to the west of Europe.

For students to "cross the bridge" from merely gathering information to improved understanding, something more has to occur beyond the act of simply absorbing data bytes—something that enables them to raise their level of knowing the information to further their understanding. Students must learn how to put the bits and pieces of information collected into a larger framework—so that they see the "big picture" and so that better understanding emerges from the pieces. Only a very few, very sophisticated students are able to make their own connections from knowing to understanding—to connect the dots, the bits of information, to see the larger picture, to comprehend the big ideas. Most students need to be taken "across the bridge" from knowing the information to better understanding by giving them specific tasks that enable them to connect the dots.

If students are better to understand, to get the big ideas, teaching must incorporate the processes of building the connections from knowing to understanding. Without their being given practice in understanding how such connections are made, without those bridges, much of the information learned is lost, and what remains leaves students with a miscellanea of unconnected dots, bereft of their meaning. There is a good reason that students forget 85 percent of the information "learned" after a two-month summer vacation.

Knowing how is a further step that takes students beyond understanding to applying what is known and what is understood—that is, putting ideas into operation. When we are able to apply understanding to the solution of problems, we advance further, to the level of knowing how. Teaching students to know how involves giving them experiences in applying knowledge to the solution of practical problems. It means, for example, enabling them to apply the principles of electrical circuitry using batteries and bulbs to make a bulb light.

The inert knowledge of the rudiments of electrical circuitry does not result, miraculously, in students' know-how (Bracey 1998; Shapiro 1994). In order for them to know how, teaching must provide the further steps so that students may cross yet another bridge to that further level of cognitive development. Teaching to *know*, to acquire information, increases students' knowledge base. Teaching to better understand enables them to make meaning from the knowledge gathered. Teaching to *know how* enables students to apply knowledge and understanding to the solution of problems.

Teaching to know how must have a means and ends connection—that is, applying what has been observed and understood. The "knowing how" proceeds from prior experiences, rather than as single, abstract projects that have no relationship to what has gone before. To achieve the goals of all three of these levels of building habits of mind, teaching must provide learning experiences in all three areas. Embedded into these three areas of cognitive development are the "thinking operations" referred to above that are more fully described in chapters 4 through 14.

The more students engage in these three levels of cognitive development, the more skilled they become in their ability to know, to understand, and to know how. Like learning to play the violin, these levels of cognitive development cannot be single experiences, but must be allowed to develop over time—thus ensuring that students become better prepared as critical and independent thinkers and learners (Wassermann 2017b).

AN INSTRUCTIONAL DESIGN FOR TEACHING FOR THINKING

The suggestions for positioning the thinking operations in a curriculum framework that allows for students to gather knowledge, to understand, and to know how, are not set in stone. Yet, from the work of many teachers using "teaching for thinking," it has become clear that the goals of knowing, understanding, and knowing how are further advanced by positioning the thinking operations in a particular progression. What follows, then, are some suggestions that come from the work of teachers over the years, to help other teachers to work toward the goals of improving students' intelligent habits of mind. (Wassermann 2009).

Thus in learning new material, students would first begin with the gathering of data through their own observations. Observations might be made, for example, through the viewing of a film or a DVD, examining an article, reading a story, a message from the internet or from a Twitter feed, a photo from Instagram, the data in a graph, or in a table, the structure of a bridge, a list of metaphors, observing and measuring the height of a "bounce" of different-sized balls, the voting record of a member of the US Senate, original historical documents, the behavior of a pet, and so on. In the best of circumstances, observing is done with some purpose—that is, students observe in order to fulfill a teacher's aims at expanding their information base.

The examples of the ways in which students can gather knowledge through observing are numerous, and many curriculum experiences, in virtually every subject area, can be introduced through requesting that students make observations. A detailed description of this operation as well as dozens of suggestions for classroom activities is found in chapter 4.

The second level in the progression requires students to process the obtained information by using the operations of comparing, classifying, looking for assumptions, suggesting hypotheses, summarizing, and interpreting data. These operations call for opportunities for students to deepen their understanding, by subjecting the information to different kinds of analyses.

At this cognitive level, students can, for example, compare two historical documents, stories, celebrity figures, two ways of solving a math problem, two presidents, warm-blooded and cold-blooded animals, the same story presented in two different newspapers, and news stories from two different media sources. They can classify historical figures, stories in a short story collection, celebrity figures, different solutions to math problems, insects, methods of transportation, video games, methods of communication, and media sources.

They can look for assumptions in televised speeches, in political slogans, newspaper editorials, advertisements, weather forecasts, in conclusions made after a science experiment, in criticisms of films and books, in "fake news," and in judgments made about a candidate for office.

They can suggest hypotheses to explain why some people need glasses, why some are allergic to different foods, why rents are more expensive in different parts of town, why ball players earn more money than teachers, what makes some people more popular than others, why some people are short and others tall, how the moon causes tides to rise and fall, why some people believe in UFOs, and why some people are superstitious.

These are just a few examples of how these operations can be used as a basis for generating higher-order curriculum tasks to promote better understanding. Many dozens of curriculum activities based on these operations are found in chapters 4 through 14.

At the third level of cognitive development, students apply what they know—putting what they know into practice. This stage includes the operations of problem solving, decision making, designing projects and investigations, making decisions, and creating and inventing.

Students can apply what they know in designing investigations to determine how they can tell that the moon affects tides, how a telephone survey can be used to gather data about preferences, how a campaign might be mounted to deal with littering in the schoolyard, how a campaign might be mounted to support recycling efforts in the school and neighborhood, how a campaign can be mounted to help students differentiate between fake and accurate reporting of the news, how money might be raised to support worthwhile causes, how elementary school students might have an effective voice in addressing world problems, such as child labor, how to demonstrate how the respiratory system works in humans and animals, and how to determine the accuracy of messages sent via the internet and social media.

The fourth level of cognitive development in the hierarchy involves students in evaluating and assessing their own work. This kind of opportunity puts them in a position where they can sharpen their skills in making thoughtful and appropriate assessments of their performance on their work. The teacher's use of higher-order questions (Bloom 1964; Raths et al. 1986) to enable this self-scrutiny encourages deeper appreciation of what is being examined, and what the perceived strengths and weaknesses are in the work. The kinds of questions that help students reflect on their work include the following:

- What was good about it?
- What would you like to have improved?
- Where does what you did need "fixing"?
- What kind of "fixing" do you think is needed?
- What new insights did you acquire from this task?
- What additional information do you need to complete the work?

Promoting this kind of personal reflection on what the student has done, revisiting what has been learned, puts a student's work through his or her own critical eye, and opens the door to further inquiry. In developing students' skills in evaluating and assessing their own work, they become more critical evaluators of what they do and how they do it. More about the kinds of teacher questions that call for students' deeper reflections on their work is found in chapter 16.

When teachers can use an instructional design that follows the sequencing of the higher-order mental operations, they can take students through the process of gathering information, making meaning of that information, and using that information in practical ways. The end result of this is that it habituates students to the process of gathering information to enable depth of understanding, before embarking on using that information and understanding to solve problems and make decisions. Student learning and thinking are the beneficiaries of this approach and the boundaries of student intelligence are advanced.

Chapter 3

Guidelines for Beginning a Teaching for Thinking Program

Teachers who introduce new topics, new programs, and new methods will appreciate the importance of orienting the students to what is to come. In that way, the students are "in on the play" and, as such, become not only knowledgeable participants, but also allies in the process. So, it would be essential that teachers make their "teaching for thinking" program clear—not only the what, but also the how and the why. There will be some important differences in a program that emphasizes thinking—and these should be explained at the outset.

For example, students' work on curriculum tasks that derive from the thinking operations is not marked or graded as other work. Instead, teachers' comments are used to highlight the strengths of students' thinking on the task, and the ways in which students might have thought more about the issues.

Students will need to know that "right answers" are not expected; what is expected is their best thinking about the issues, or the topics. These responses should be based in data that come not only from students' experiences, but also from texts and other sources that provide reliable information.

As with many thinking tasks, there may be several "good" responses that vary from student to student, and it is often of benefit to call on students to examine these various and different responses so that they may consider their wisdom and appropriateness.

Many teachers have found that one way to initiate work on a thinking task is with small group work. When students can confer with each other, it helps them to formulate their ideas in a small and safe context. Of course, small group work does not necessarily become productive after only a single or a few trials. Like other skills, working in small groups becomes more productive after practice, and reflection on practice.

But the benefit of students working together to examine the task, and to formulate ideas, and then to use this experience as an introduction to the whole class discussion that follows can be very productive. Of course, before beginning small group work, it is helpful to specify what is required and to make specific the teacher's expectations.

Some of these include, for example, careful and respectful listening to the opinions of others no matter how different they are from one's own, taking notes that represent the voices of the group so that all students who wish to be heard have a turn, as well as ensuring that no one monopolizes the discussion. At a more sophisticated level, students may ask each other about the reliability and accuracy of the data behind their responses to the task work.

Some teachers have found it helpful to introduce a particular operation before committing students to a curriculum task that calls for work based on that operation. This might be more important for students who have not had much experience working on tasks that require higher-order mental processing.

So, for example, before students begin their first task that calls for observing to be done, teachers might introduce the operation of Observing—and make clear what is involved; what the expectations are; what it means to "sharpen one's senses" and see, hear, and perceive, as a way to gather knowledge, and to differentiate between what is fact and what is speculation; and what is true and what is "truthiness." Some examples of thoughtful observations might be presented and discussed.

A more complete discussion for each operation is found in the chapters that follow.

Teachers' classroom experiences with the thinking operations have also taught that there is no single "right way" to begin and carry out an approach to curriculum that emphasizes higher-order thinking and includes the thinking operations. There is no evidence to suggest that one must begin with "observing" and follow through the hierarchy described above.

The sky doesn't fall if students begin their work with comparing or classifying activities. The school does not tremble if teachers choose to bypass small group work in favor of individual or whole class work. Teachers are wonderfully creative and inventive and will find their own best ways to work with their own classes, for teachers know best what works for which students and how to put these ideas into practice.

With all of these caveats and provisos, the following guidelines to aid and abet teachers considering the implementation of teaching for thinking in their classrooms are offered:

(a) Decide on the subject area that best allows, for your class, an introduction to teaching for thinking.

(b) Develop an activity, with an emphasis on one of the thinking operations, in a subject area that feels most comfortable to you. (Many suggestions are offered in the subsequent chapters to help you either in making your choice or in developing one of your own.)

(c) Make sure the students understand the nature of the operation—that is, what is required as they tackle the task.

(d) Present the task to the students. Allow them adequate time for their questions.

(e) Students may begin their work in small groups, or as individuals. If small group work is chosen, make sure the students understand the criteria for productive group work.

(f) Ask the students to record their responses in a notebook or paper, or, if they choose, a laptop or tablet computer.

(g) Make sure the students have sufficient time to complete the task.

(h) Ask students to share their responses in a whole class discussion. Use higher-order questions and reflective responses (see chapter 16) in helping them to reexamine their ideas and to probe for deeper meaning.

(i) When the activity and the "debriefing" of the activity are finished, invite students' comments about the nature of their experience with "teaching for thinking." Ask them to make suggestions for their further engagement with subsequent teaching for thinking tasks.

(j) Use at least one thinking activity per day in the curriculum area of your choice.

NOW THE FUN BEGINS

The first three chapters of this book present the basic principles that are the foundation of a "teaching for thinking" program, as well as offering some important reasons why such a curriculum emphasis is so urgent in these times of an overload of truthiness and disinformation. Chapters 4 through 14 present detailed descriptions of the thinking operations and offer many ideas for curriculum tasks that can be drawn from them, across curriculum areas and grade levels.

In the last section of the book, chapters 15–17, suggestions are presented for dealing with students' deeply entrenched beliefs, how higher-order questions and reflective responses encourage further inquiry, how a teacher-student interactive dialogue plays out, and, last, how teachers may evaluate students' work in their development of more intelligent habits of mind.

As teachers embark on this exciting adventure into promoting students' intelligent habits of mind, it is helpful to remember what Socrates famously said at his trial for impiety and the corruption of youth: "The unexamined life is not worth living."

Section II

Chapter 4

Introduction to Observing

There is now a large collection of articles and books (e.g., the *Journal of Applied Psychology*, the *Stanford Law Review*, and the *Scientific American*, to name a few) that attest to the unreliability of eyewitness accounts of criminal situations. What these researchers reveal is that there are many factors that influence accurate observations of events and persons, and that when the observers are asked to recall what they have seen, the results are often ambiguous, sometimes contradictory, and more often false.

There are many factors that can diminish the accuracy of observations, and these include the emotional state of the observer during the time the observation occurred, the lack of distinct characteristics of the person or place being observed, and the built-in bias of the observer, who filters what is seen through his or her personal reference points—tending to see what he or she "wants" to see, rather than what is actually there.

Observing, while not considered a sophisticated skill, is actually a trained ability. We don't think of it as such, because it is something we do every day, and in many contexts. To observe accurately, however, depends upon our ability to do this free from personal bias, and to be aware of any emotional factors that might influence what we are seeing or hearing. It's a mistake to consider it easy.

That it is an important skill is not in question; the more accurately we are able to observe, the more we are able to discriminate what is there, and make meaning of what we see and hear with greater accuracy. The cognitive challenge in observing is to learn to differentiate between what is actually seen, or heard, and what is "filled in" or distorted through the lens of personal bias. The more accurate the observation, the closer it comes to fact. Observing then becomes an important tool in acquiring accurate information, in being able to differentiate between what is true and what is imagined to be true. It is a part of the process of responding with more accuracy to what is going on in the world.

In sharing our observations with others, we have an opportunity to become more aware of our "blind spots" and the "blind spots" of others. We learn to see what we had not seen before. We develop greater discrimination and become more thoughtful.

We must be sure, however, that the observing activities we create for students are worthwhile, and that students are engaged in observing "what's important" and not activities that deal in trivia or in matters of little consequence. There should be important reasons to make observations.

The most telling anecdote about teaching students to observe comes from *Louis Agassiz as a Teacher* (Cooper 1917). Agassiz taught graduate students in biology at Harvard University and the following incident comes from the reflections of one of his former students.

It was more than fifteen years ago that I entered the laboratory of Professor Agassiz and told him that I had enrolled my name in the Scientific School as a student of natural history. He asked me a few questions about my object in coming, my antecedents generally, the mode in which I afterwards proposed to use the knowledge I might acquire, and finally whether I wished to study any special branch. To the latter I replied that, while I wished to be well grounded in all departments of zoology, I purposed to devote myself specially to insects.

"When do you wish to begin?" he asked.

"Now," I replied.

This seemed to please him, and with an energetic "Very well," he reached from a shelf a huge jar of specimen in yellow alcohol.

"Take this fish," said he, "and look at it; we call it a haemulon; by and by I will ask what you have seen."

With that he left me, but in a moment returned with explicit instructions as to the care of the object entrusted to me.

"No man is fit to be a naturalist," said he, "who does not know how to take care of specimens."

I was to keep the fish before me in a tin tray, and occasionally moisten the surface with alcohol from the jar, always taking care to replace the stopper tightly. Those were not the days of ground glass stoppers and elegantly shaped exhibition jars; all the old students will recall the huge neckless glass bottles with their leaky, wax besmirched corks, half eaten by insects, and begrimed with cellar dust. Entomology was a cleaner science than ichthyology, but the example of the Professor, who had unhesitatingly plunged to the bottom of the jar to produce the fish was infectious; and though this alcohol had "a very ancient and fishlike smell," I really dared not show any aversion within these sacred precincts, and treated the alcohol as though it were pure water. Still I was conscious of a passing feeling of disappointment, for gazing at a fish did not commend itself to an ardent entomologist. My friends at home, too, were annoyed when they discovered that no amount of eau-de-Cologne would drown the perfume which haunted me like a shadow.

In ten minutes I had seen all that could be seen in that fish, and started in search of the Professor—who had, however, left the Museum; and when I returned, after lingering over some of the odd animals stored in the upper apartment, my specimen was dry all over. I dashed the fluid over the fish as if to resuscitate the beast from a fainting fit, and looked with anxiety for a return of the normal sloppy appearance. This little excitement over, nothing was to be done but to return to a steadfast gaze at my mute companion. Half an hour passed—an hour—another hour; the fish began to look loathsome. I turned it over and around; looked it in the face—ghastly; from behind, beneath, above, sideways, at a three-quarters' view—just as ghastly. I was in despair; at an early hour I concluded that lunch was necessary; so with infinite relief, the fish was carefully replaced in the jar, and for an hour I was free.

On my return, I learned that Professor Agassiz had gone and would not return for several hours. Slowly I drew forth that hideous fish, and with a feeling of desperation again looked at it. I might not use a magnifying glass; instruments of all kinds were interdicted. My two hands, my two eyes, and the fish. It seemed a most limited field. I pushed my finger down its throat to feel how sharp the teeth were. I began to count the scales in the different rows until I was convinced that that was nonsense. At last a happy thought struck me—I would draw the fish; and now with surprise I began to discover new features in the creature. Just then, the Professor returned.

"That is right," said he, "a pencil is one of the best of eyes. I am glad to notice, too, that you keep your specimen wet and your bottle corked."

With these encouraging words, he added:

"Well, what is it like?

He listened attentively to my brief rehearsal of the structure of parts whose names were still unknown to me: the fringed gill-arches and movable operculum; the pores of the head, fleshy lips and lidless eyes; the lateral line, the spinous fins and forked tail, the compressed and arched body. When I had finished, he waited as if expecting more, and then, with an air or disappointment:

"You have not looked very carefully; why," he continued more earnestly, "you haven't even seen one of the most conspicuous features of the animal, which is as plainly before your eyes as the fish itself; look again, look again!" and he left me to my misery.

I was piqued; I was mortified. Still more of that wretched fish! But now I set myself to my task with a will, and discovered one new thing after another until I saw how just the Professor's criticism had been. The afternoon passed quickly; and when, toward its close, the Professor inquired:

"Do you see it yet?"

"No," I replied, "I am certain I do not, but I see how little I saw before."

"That is next best," said he earnestly, "but I won't hear you now; put away your fish and go home; perhaps you will be ready with a better answer in the morning. I will examine you before you look at the fish."

This was disconcerting. Not only must I think of my fish all night, studying, without the object before me, what this unknown but most visible feature might be; but also, without reviewing my new discoveries, I must give an exact account of them the next day. I had a bad memory; so I walked home by the Charles River in a distracted state, with my two perplexities.

The cordial greeting from the Professor the next morning was reassuring; here was a man who seemed to be quite as anxious as I that I should see for myself what he saw.

"Do you perhaps mean," I asked, "that the fish has symmetrical sides with paired organs?"

His thoroughly pleased "Of course! Of course!" repaid the wakeful hours of the previous night. After he had discoursed most happily and enthusiastically—as he always did—upon the importance of this point, I ventured to ask what I should do next.

"Oh, look at your fish!" he said, and left me again to my own devices. In a little more than an hour he returned and heard my new catalogue.

"Oh, that is good, that is good!" he repeated, "but that is not all, go on." And so for three long days he placed that fish before my eyes, forbidding me to look at anything else, or to use any artificial aid. "Look, look, look" was his repeated injunction.

This was the best entomological lesson I ever had—a lesson whose influence has extended to the details of every subject I study; a legacy the Professor has left to me, as he has left it to many others, of inestimable value, which we could not buy with which we cannot part.

The fourth day a second fish of the same group was placed beside the first, and I was bidden to point out the resemblances and differences between the two; another and another followed, until the entire family lay before me, and a whole legion of jars covered the table and surrounding shelves; the odor had become a pleasant perfume; and even now, the sight of an old, six-inch, worm eaten cork brings fragrant memories.

The whole group of haemulons was thus brought in review; and, whether engaged upon the dissection of the internal organs, the preparations and examination of the bony framework, or the description of the various parts, Agassiz's training in the method of observing facts and their orderly arrangement was ever accompanied by the urgent exhortation not to be content with them.

"Facts are stupid things," he would say, "until brought into connection with some general law."

At the end of eight months, it was almost with reluctance that I left these friends and turned to insects; but what I had gained by this outside experience has been of greater value than years of later investigation in my favorite groups (Cooper 1917).

There is also the Sir Arthur Conan Doyle story, *The Adventure of the Blue Carbuncle*, in which Sherlock Holmes gives the recently found Derby hat to his companion, Dr. Watson, and asks what can be seen. Watson examines the hat and tells Holmes that he can see nothing. Whereupon Holmes exhorts him, "You see but do not observe!" And he proceeds to give an extensive and detailed observation of what can be seen, from the size, the quality of the material, the way the hat has deteriorated, and the bits of candlewax on the brim. From his observations, Holmes was able to deduce the nature of the man's occupation, his relations with his wife, and the fact that there was no gaslight in his home. There is much wisdom to be gained from careful and detailed observation if we train ourselves to look carefully and study what is there to be seen.

CLASSROOM APPLICATIONS

You don't have to be a teacher of zoology, a professor at Harvard, or a Sherlock Holmes to engage students in observing activities in which they learn to gather data from sustained examination of what can be seen. This can be accomplished at any educational level—and in virtually any subject area. There are literally hundreds of ways in which students can gather data by observing.

For example, students can observe by viewing animals and plants in their natural habitat, or in museums, aquariums, and zoos. A walk around the neighborhood can lead to observations about housing, about gardens, about traffic, and about how many and what kinds of people are seen and what they are doing. The natural sciences are particularly fruitful subject areas for making observations, for example, studying bones and/or shells, skeletons, birds in their natural habitats or in photos, horses, farm animals, pets, skins, feathers, fur, microbes, and insects.

The physical sciences can offer observations of light and shadow, balances, thermometers, parachutes, sounds, wind energy, static electricity, kites, friction and inertia, pulleys, various tools, time, magnets, and bouncing balls. Mathematical observations can include measurements, money, counting, shapes, graphs, volume and capacity, and time. In the language arts, students may observe characters in a play, or story, the nature of narrative, different ways in which words are used to express ideas, and the construction of sentences and paragraphs.

Social studies is a rich subject area for observing and tasks may include observations of people doing certain jobs; viewing and or listening to actual events being telecast; examining internet and social media postings; television, newspaper, and magazine advertisements; photos in history textbooks; posters that advertise political campaigns; fashions in clothing that change over the years; transportation; and ways in which we communicate via different media. How many students, can one imagine, have actually examined, in close observation, the Bill of Rights? The Pledge of Allegiance? The Declaration of Independence? The Constitution? Wouldn't these be productive areas for intense examination?

Observing photos of structures, like the pyramids, the Coliseum in Rome, the Hoover Dam, the Terra Cotta Warriors, the ceiling of the Sistine Chapel, a Rube Goldberg machine, the Alhambra Palace, and the Bayeux Tapestry, is more than helpful for sharpening observing skills, but can also shed light on the workmanship, the structural designs of the age, and, of course, the history of the periods they represent. Observing famous works of art—from the primitive designs on caves to the more modern work of artists—is another set of examples of how observing activities can lead to new insights and awareness.

MAKING OBSERVATIONS ABOUT SOCIAL ISSUES

Current events and the news coming from various sources offer rich opportunities for students to make observations that would be of great benefit in their understanding of what is going in their immediate communities, in the country, and in the world. These would be of particular significance because they would invite students to become more discerning, more tuned into the differences between what is fact and what is opinion, what are data, what are value judgments, and what is disinformation.

Using internet sources to check for accuracy of information, like PolitiFact, FactCheck.org, and the Sunlight Foundation, to name only three, is helpful in pointing students to the ways and means of sifting through what is real and what is fake. Sharpening students' skills as observers provides them with the grounding in using intelligent habits of mind to become more in tune with reality.

Many of the examples offered below may be more suitable for more mature students, but some can surely be adapted for use with younger groups. In developing or selecting tasks that call for observations to be made, it is a good idea to begin with an identification of the "big ideas"—that is, what does the teacher believe is the central issue of what she or he wants the students to observe, and therefore to gather data about. In newspapers, textbooks, and other sources, there will be many articles, graphs, tables, maps, films, photos, and internet presentations that may be used as a basis for making observations.

The caveat in using or adapting relevant social issues as curriculum activities in which students are asked to make observations is that they are, more than often, "emotionally loaded"—and teachers are put on alert in their use— not that they should shy away from them, but that they should be prepared that they may open a Pandora's Box of feelings. Holding students' views to what is observable fact is one way of maintaining thoughtful and significant discussions.

Some suggestions for making observations about social issues are the following:

- Graphs that show income inequality in the United States
- Newspaper articles or photos describing extreme weather conditions
- Photos of recent Ku Klux Klan parades and marches
- Illustrations of the widespread use of mobile phones
- Advertisements urging purchase of certain products in newspapers, magazines, and the internet
- Articles or essays about immigration in various countries
- Documentary films about social issues
- Graphs that show the recipients of the Nobel Peace Prize in the past twenty years
- Stories or essays about the impact of social media on teens
- Stories, articles, or graphs that discuss or show the decline in employment in certain key industries
- Photos or articles about the homeless
- Photos or stories about life on a Native American reservation
- Stories, photos, or graphs that demonstrate the continued incidence of racial inequality
- Stories, photos, or graphs that demonstrate the rise of obesity in young people
- Stories, articles, or photos that show how lobbyists influence the electoral process in the United States
- Photo or illustration of the Vietnam War Memorial in Washington, DC
- Photo that shows the retreating British Army at Dunkirk in the spring of 1940
- Map of Africa that shows the countries that had been "colonized" by European rulers
- Map that shows the European countries that had been invaded by Nazi Germany
- Photos that show young black students being admitted to a previously all-white school in the American South

The possibilities are vast. But it is important to remember that observing is not an idle task; students observe with purpose—as a way of gathering data to learn something more, to begin their understanding of what is seen, of what is there. It is the first step in leading to increased knowledge and better understanding.

Any of the above suggestions for curriculum tasks can be shaped to fit the needs of primary, intermediate, secondary, and even postsecondary students—depending on the nature and kind of challenge the observations pose and, of course, the wording of the task. But more important, they may serve as examples for teachers to develop observing tasks from their own curriculum guides.

It is a given that primary, intermediate, secondary, and postsecondary students will vary in the sophistication of their observations and this is expected. At first, observations may be meager and superficial, as was demonstrated in the short essay about Louis Agassiz's student. But over time, as students grow in their observational skills, they will become more astute, more thoughtful, more accurate, and more knowledgeable, appreciating more the importance of using astute observing skills to gather data.

In the hierarchy of thinking operations, becoming a more discriminating observer is a beginning step—the step in which data are gathered, leading to more sophisticated analyses, that is, the ways in which data are analyzed and understood.

As students present their observations in a whole class discussion, their ideas are further examined through questions that ask them to think further, to "defend" what they believe to have seen, and to support their ideas with data from their observations. Questions may be such as the following:

- Can you tell me a little more about where you see that?
- You may be using data that go beyond what is seen/heard. Can you tell me where you got that idea?
- Are you making some assumptions? Can you show me where that observation is supported by the data?
- Tell me about the kind of fact-checking you have done to determine the truth of those observations.
- Are there some value judgments implied in your statement? Can you rephrase your observation by eliminating the judgments and staying with the data?

More suggestions using questions that call for deeper and more intelligent examination of observed data are found in chapter 17.

SCENES FROM THE CLASSROOM

The Grade 3 students were working in small study groups, examining a photo of a large fish. They were given ample opportunity to work in these small groups, to discuss their observations, and to interact with each other about what they had observed. After the small group work had concluded, the teacher called the whole group together and asked for their observations. These they eagerly volunteered and the teacher, using reflective responses and higher order questions, worked with their observations and attempted to keep their observations "on track." Carl was next to offer his ideas:

Carl: See these things here (he points to the photo). These are the fins. They used to have feet, but the feet turned into fins.

Teacher: (Misinterpreting, tries to say it back) So the fins turned into feet.

Carl: NO! The feet turned into fins.

Teacher: (Now a bit confused, looks down at her feet and asks): Hmm—do you think that could happen to me? My feet would turn into fins?

Carl: No! It takes about a hundred years.

Chapter 5

Introduction to Comparing

The operation of Comparing takes a step beyond Observing—since comparing requires thoughtful observations to discern similarities and differences. Even the most routine examination of what is mentally required in comparing reveals that the mind needs to "work"—one needs to engage the mind in order to be able to apprehend what is alike and what is dissimilar—searching out the relationships that one item has to another, seeking points of agreement and disagreement.

A requirement to keep close to the data in the items to be compared teaches students to become more vigilant in making unwarranted assumptions and more cautious about inserting personal bias in what is being compared. As students gain experience with comparing, they learn that what, at first glance, seems to be alike may not, in fact, be alike at all.

Comparing requires thoughtful examination of material—the mind working to establish the comparative reference points. What's important in generating tasks requiring comparisons is that students work with items of relevance or significance, for when comparing is done superficially, or only for the sake of doing it, it can be almost as dull as a routine lesson in memorizing Latin declensions.

But when there is real purpose in the analysis of similarities and differences, where there is real motive for this differentiation, the task is more than interesting. It becomes stimulating for both teachers and students. On the other hand, as Raths (1986, 6) has suggested, "It should perhaps be noted that comparisons of even trivial objects probably yield more in motivation and content learning than assignments that put great emphasis on recall alone."

In making observations, students usually work from information that is on hand—viewing or listening to what is readily seen or heard. But when students compare, it may also be the case that the data must be recalled, or perceived, or evoked—and that gives more latitude for "reading in" or assuming what is there, and more reason for students to learn to be more cautious about making assumptions that go beyond the data as well as making value judgments that are far afield from what is observed and apprehended.

While assumptions and value judgments are not errors, what is important is that students learn to be aware of them and not confuse assumptions and value judgments with facts. In other words, "truthiness" has no place in data-based comparisons. See, for example, the paragraph at the end of chapter 4, an anecdote about observations and assumptions.

Searching through the subject areas offers extensive opportunities for students to exercise their minds in making comparisons. Comparing activities are not suggested as alternates to learning what is important, but, in fact, they provide a means of discerning what is important about what is being studied. Activities in which students are asked to compare give them insight into the big ideas of the subjects being studied.

Students who have not had opportunities to engage in comparing activities in the past may be helped by some introductions to more simple comparing tasks—making clear that what is called for is the identification of what is observably similar and what is different. Some examples of thoughtfully designed comparisons may be helpful as starting points.

It is not unusual for students to begin comparing items by noting more insignificant details, but with experience in the process, they graduate to more sophisticated awareness of what is similar and what is different. In any event, it may be helpful to introduce comparing activities to the uninitiated with more simple tasks before engaging them with tasks that require much more mature awareness and experience.

The happy result from students who engage in comparing activities is that more often than not, important insights are revealed, and, of course, students become more adept at using comparing as a means of making more informed decisions.

CLASSROOM APPLICATIONS

Traditional school subject areas are rife with possibilities for students to compare and a few are suggested below as examples of what may be distilled from the curriculum. No differentiations are offered for specific grade levels, as comparing activities may be shaped and reshaped to encompass several grades, depending on the background of experience, the maturity, and learning levels of the students.

So, in fact, postsecondary students can as easily be asked to compare the American Revolution with the French Revolution as can secondary students.

Even intermediate students of a certain maturity can make such comparisons, although the results are likely to be less sophisticated in insight and depth of knowledge. What is important in selecting items for comparison is the level of maturity of the students and their background of experience with the area of study. It would not be productive for students or for their thinking processes to be asked to compare World War I with World War II if their background knowledge and experiences with these two major events of the twentieth century were only rudimentary.

Of course, comparisons should emerge from a body of data, rather than from recall, so that the experience can lead to richer and more informed insights into what is similar and what is different.

Some suggestions for comparing activities are the following:

- Two methods of solving a math problem
- Two neighborhoods
- Two methods of transportation
- Two types of government
- Two geographical areas
- Two rivers
- Two heads of state
- Two stories by the same author
- Two stories by different authors
- Celsius and Fahrenheit
- Two types of bridges
- Tablet computers and laptop computers
- Facebook and FaceTime
- Skype and FaceTime
- GPS and flat maps
- iPhones and landlines
- YouTube videos and commercial films
- Information from the internet and information from an encyclopedia or map
- Martin Luther King Jr. and Malcolm X
- Martin Luther King Jr. and Gandhi
- Huey Long and Joseph McCarthy
- World War I and World War II
- North Korea and South Korea
- Mao Zedong and Stalin
- Newspapers and TV news
- E-mail messages and Tweets
- A computer and a smartphone
- Characters in a story, for example, Jean Valjean and Inspector Javert

- Alfred Dreyfus and Mata Hari
- Santa Claus and the Great Pumpkin
- July 4th and Canada Day
- Decimals and fractions
- Roman numerals and Arabic numerals
- The Gobi desert and the Sahara desert
- Chimpanzees and dogs
- Bees and mosquitoes
- Apartments and single-family homes
- Navajos and Apaches
- Soccer and baseball

The following are some examples of more sophisticated comparing activities in the social studies that are more sensitive and might give rise to some extreme views—and, as a consequence, should be undertaken with that in mind:

- Comparing similarities and differences between the events that led to World War I and those that led to World War II, from a British perspective
- Comparing similarities and differences between US immigration policies in 1900 and 2017
- Comparing similarities and differences between the cultural constraints imposed on women in the United States in the 1920s and today
- Comparing similarities and differences between federal support to the economically disadvantaged during the years of the Great Depression and today
- Comparing similarities and differences in the way news is gathered today and in the early twentieth century
- Comparing the similarities and differences between the Bill of Rights and the Magna Carta
- Comparing different claims about climate change
- Comparing electric cars with gasoline-powered cars
- Comparing self-driven cars with driverless cars
- Comparing the action of Rosa Parks to that of Nat Turner's slave rebellion
- Comparing the presidency of Abraham Lincoln with that of Lyndon B. Johnson
- Comparing Margaret Thatcher with Ronald Reagan
- Comparing drug addiction treatments in Portugal to those in the United States
- Comparing Fox News with CNN
- Comparing women's employment opportunities in the workforce during World War II and in the 1950s

- Comparing incidents of extreme weather conditions in the United States in 2017 and 1917
- Comparing the reasons for the US engagement in the Vietnam War and the Korean War
- Comparing the leadership of Stalin and Hitler
- Comparing the aftereffects of the Russian Revolution with the French Revolution
- Comparing governments under Bolshevism and Nazism

These are only a very few suggestions for engaging students in comparing activities. It is hoped that these examples will motivate teachers to look into their own curriculum guides to see what events, issues, and ideas will lend themselves easily to the creation of comparing tasks. However, it should be cautioned that when comparing is done with a real purpose, when there is a real motive for searching for the like and the unlike, the process proves to be not only interesting but also an active mental engagement that leads to some increased awareness and understanding.

When students are presenting their comparative ideas, questions that call for deeper thinking of the issues can be raised. For example:

- Can you tell me a little more about how you came to see those as differences?
- What do you suppose explains some of those differences?
- How do the differences help you to understand a little more about _____?
- What makes you think that is true? What data do you have to support that idea?
- Have you made an assumption here? What data support it?

And sometimes it is helpful, in the aftermath of the discussions, for the students to reexamine their comparisons, and make any changes they consider appropriate. Thus, active mental processing continues.

At the very least, students sharpening their comparing skills are less likely to accept what is seen, heard, or read at face value—such an important attribute in discerning and making meaning of what is going on in the world.

SCENES FROM THE CLASSROOM

Bob, a grade 4 student who had been identified as a boy who was prone to leap to conclusions, make unwarranted assumptions, and was dogmatic in his assertions, was introduced to comparing with an activity that asked him to look for similarities and differences in two approaches to teaching reading—Group Reading and Self-Reading (both of which he had experienced in his school years). He made the following comparisons:

Self-Reading

1. *You can read better.*
2. *You pick your own book whenever you want.*
3. *You read as much as you want.*
4. *You can read A.M. or P.M.*
5. *You can stop in the book whenever you want.*
6. *You can tell others about the book.*
7. *You have a conference with the teacher anytime you want.*

Group Reading

1. *You have a hard time reading.*
2. *You have to read the book you're given and read it at a certain time.*
3. *You can read only a certain amount.*
4. *You have to read it in the morning.*
5. *You read the whole book, whether you like it or not.*
6. *You can't sell a book because the other children have already read it.*
7. *You don't have a conference with the teacher.*

On the basis of his comparison, Bob concluded that the items he had included in his comparison showed how much he preferred "Self-Reading" over "Group Reading," and this was an important insight for him.

Chapter 6

Introduction to Classifying

The operation of classifying requires that we identify certain characteristics of items that allow them to be grouped in a way in which the items relate to each other. Why is this a higher-order mental activity? To observe a group of items, to consider and reflect on how they are associated with each other, asks for the identification of particular attributes of the items—discerning, observing, and comparing—and then understanding how certain attributes are connected. It involves analysis and synthesis.

When students become more skilled in classifying, it allows them to deepen their understanding and make meaning of their experiences. It encourages them to make order out of their world, to think on their own, and to come to their own conclusions. Becoming adept at classifying contributes to students' maturity.

Classifying is an extension of observing and comparing. As students discern similarities and differences in a collection of items, they assign these items to groups on the basis of size, form, structure, effect, or some other criterion that has been discerned. What classifying requires is the conceptualization or the creation of taxonomies. Subjects such as botany and natural science are essentially huge taxonomic systems. A person who has difficulty with classifying may be showing signs of inability to conceptualize, to see relationships, and to think.

From early childhood, classifying is the way in which we organize our lives and thereby make sense of our world. We continue to "receive" the outside world through expanding our conceptualizations. Although there are no "right" or "wrong" ways to classify items, classifications are "more correct" if they serve the purpose of the grouping. And, of course, the groupings should make sense.

Rothstein (Raths et al. 1986, 105) has written that "the process of abstracting is basic to the processes of thought. In extracting or abstracting a single characteristic as the basis of classifying, one has to be aware that one is necessarily omitting. Classifying or categorizing cannot be done without such omission."

Classifying can be seen as a convenience, and although there can be considerable variation among classification schemes, the way one classifies is neither arbitrary nor a truth. Rothstein (Raths et al. 1986, 105) goes on to state that "any political, racial, religious, national, geographic, social, generational, sex or physical characteristic grouping can be a force for ill will if its stance is primarily adversarial. Some of the greatest conflicts have arisen in connection with classifications of human beings that have hardened into rigidity."

Teachers are cautioned that certain classifications of ethnic groups may tilt students to prejudicial positions, serving negative and unhealthy purposes. Should that occur, it would be important to address any deep-rooted prejudices that emerge from such classifications. The best ways of doing this is through the use of higher-order questions that bring unfounded and biased points of view into the light and under deeper and more rational examination. In other words, the use of classifying exercises can bring unhealthy and prejudicial notions under more critical scrutiny.

There are well-established taxonomies—and through them we can see how classification systems illuminate our thinking and understanding. For example, there are classifications in law (felony, offense, misdemeanor), in parts of speech (noun, verb, adjective), and in the biological sciences (animal, plant). However, what is intended here is for teachers to use curriculum guides and subject area content to see where and how students can develop classification systems that further their thinking about the big ideas and important issues in the content, and thereby enrich their understanding.

Some examples of potential classification activities are suggested below— but again, these are only illustrations of how students, at any grade level, can be asked to engage in classifying activities.

CLASSROOM APPLICATIONS

In the early grades, children already do some classifying when they are asked to put away their blocks and paints, for example. The big blocks go into that bin and the smaller ones into the other bin. The red paints and green paints and blue paints all have their own jars and storage places. At home, children know that socks go into this drawer and underwear into that drawer, forks into that slot and spoons into the other.

But more advanced tasks involving classifying and sorting can occur within curriculum frameworks. What is important in asking students to create categories is that there is some purpose to the request to classify, and that there is a clear, conceptual relationship to the arrangement of items into groups. When selecting a classifying activity, it is a good idea to begin with the list of items to be classified, and then checking the list to see if most of the relevant items have been included, before a classification system is set up.

- States of the United States
- Countries in Asia, Europe, Africa, and South America
- Heads of states and countries
- Social classes
- Types of recreation for children and/or adults
- Types of governments
- Mountain ranges
- Types of schools
- Types of clothing
- Types of entertainment for children/for adults
- Types of communication systems
- Types of housing/residences
- Ways of transporting goods
- Fears
- Imports and exports
- Wars
- Insects
- Composers
- Types of music
- Musical instruments
- Tools
- Parts of the body
- Countries of the world
- Sports
- Skeletal bones
- Food
- Beverages
- Fish
- Sounds
- Plants
- Different ways of measuring
- Birds
- Colors
- Garbage (or items in the school trash)

- Metals
- Geometrical shapes
- Jobs and work
- News sources
- Video games
- Vegetables
- Holidays
- National monuments
- Works of art
- Recreational activities
- Sources of energy
- Methods of transportation
- Native American tribes
- Cutting-edge technologies
- Emperors of the Roman Empire
- World War II generals
- World War I battles
- Groups of immigrants to the United States in the past 100 years
- Hurricanes of the past fifty years
- Earthquakes of the past fifty years
- Nobel Peace Prize recipients

As a culminating activity, it may be helpful to ask the students to share their classification systems and then to inquire, using higher-order questions and responses, as to which system is preferred, and why. Which system is more helpful? More productive? Allows for greater insight? This is a way to engage students in the examination and reexamination of the process of classifying and illuminating what has been learned and what insights have been gained in the process.

The end results of classifying are that new insights are discovered from the classification; we learn more and understand more when we sort items according to what we consider to be their common characteristics.

SCENES FROM THE CLASSROOM

Eddie, a grade 6 boy, was asked to make a list of the things he had a deep aversion to. He listed thirty-one items:

1. *Classical music*
2. *Communism*
3. *Long car rides*

4. *Corduroy*
5. *Velvet*
6. *Grouchy people*
7. *Bossy people*
8. *Spinach*
9. *Plums*
10. *Peaches*
11. *Peanut butter*
12. *Untidiness*
13. *Love stories*
14. *Small print*
15. *Bullies*
16. *Pies*
17. *Physical discomforts*
18. *Short hair*
19. *Greasy hair*
20. *Poor manners*
21. *Gardening*
22. *Housework*
23. *Red hair*
24. *Rude people*
25. *Sauerkraut*
26. *Pickles*
27. *Sad music*
28. *Diseases*
29. *Shots*
30. *Bad teachers*
31. *People who wear perfume*

When he had completed his list, he was asked to classify the items and when he had done that he wrote the following analysis:

My prejudices are few but the thing that disturbs me most is "Characteristics of People." (Here he was referring to a category which he had set up.) In my life I have come across many types of people such as grouchy people, bossy people, rude people, etc., but when I stop to think, I find I have judged some of my prejudices very unfairly, such as red hair. This bothers me badly because it is not the person's fault but the person was born that way. Doing this work made me stop and think about my prejudices and I find that I was very very wrong, therefore I think that this assignment was very interesting and good.

Chapter 7

Introduction to Suggesting Hypotheses

When faced with a puzzling dilemma, we may use hypotheses to try to figure out some potential solutions. Hypotheses represent educated guesses. They are tentative and provisional—"tools" that suggest possible courses of action. Sometimes, hypotheses operate as guides to explain why something will work or not work. As students learn to use hypothesizing, they learn to be less impulsive about jumping to conclusions based on inadequate data. They gain in their ability to be more self-reliant, more independent, and more competent in working out solutions to problems they face.

We may have hypotheses about solutions; we may have them about sources of data, about the length of time it would take to work on a problem, about the availability of resources, about the competence of a person to do a particular job, and about a particular investment in a company's success.

We may have hypotheses about why some students are bullies, about the potential success of an anti-bullying program, about the gentrification of neighborhoods, about the preservation of our National Parks, about the benefits of using organic food, about the internment of Japanese Americans during World War II, about the annihilation of the Native populations in the United States during the westward movement, about the kind of thinking that led to the outbreak of World War I, about the tenacity of Jim Crow laws in the American south after the Civil War, and about the "silent" rules that enforce sexism, racial discrimination, and segregated schools. These are only a few examples of how students may be engaged in generating hypotheses to explain extraordinary events and problems.

One way of introducing the operation of hypothesizing to students is to present a "real-life" problem to them and ask them to generate some hypotheses, or explanations, for why this would occur. For example, can students think of some reasons to explain why it is that two of the students in a particular class have such a hard time working productively together? When the teacher puts these two students into the same group, they almost always get into a fight. What might be some reasons for this? What are some explanations for it?

The children might be asked to think of as many possible explanations as they can. A list is made of the hypotheses. This may be the beginning of their understanding that generating hypotheses is one way in which we attempt to answer a question that is puzzling us—and by examining the list of hypotheses, we begin to see which are more viable and which are the better potential explanations. If we were to proceed to test our hypotheses, which would be the most likely place to begin?

As they embark on the developmental process of learning about generating hypotheses, students grow to understand that hypotheses are not answers but rather speculations. They ask students to conjecture about the facts, use their best intelligence to explain, and, thus, to further their understanding and their ability to reason rationally and with sound judgment. The more students can be engaged in searching for credible hypotheses to explain, to examine dilemmas, the more they are building their habits of intelligent thinking and reasoning and the less likely are they to fall into the trap of proposing an "off the cuff" conclusion to explain a problematic situation.

The primary objective in giving students experiences with hypothesizing is to help them understand and consider the variety of possibilities, which may be involved in arriving at an explanation of a phenomenon. Instead of impulsively leaping to conclusions about what is wrong, or what the problem is all about, they develop the ability to suspend judgment, to take a long glance, to consider possibilities, and to suggest theories. The process of working the mind to step back and consider, rather than to blindly accept, is engaged.

To introduce students to the concept of hypothesizing is not difficult. Most of them learn quickly, and many of them see this learned skill as a benefit to them in working through problems.

As a starting point, students need to understand that hypotheses are "educated guesses"—tentative explanations of something they have observed, or have been told about. After an initial introduction, it is usually a good idea to give students several examples in which they are asked to arrive together at a number of hypotheses to explain a given situation. This type of whole group activity may help the teacher to see how well the concept is being learned and which students may need additional help in formulating hypotheses.

In addition, students can be helped to understand that often many possibilities, or hypotheses, may be suggested for a problem and that it may take further examination or testing of a hypothesis before they can ascertain which is the more appropriate. Implied in hypothesizing, therefore, is the notion of being able to test the various hypotheses presented. It is also important to note that more than one hypothesis may provide an appropriate explanation for a given dilemma.

Also helpful in promoting the idea that a hypothesis is a reasonable possibility, it is suggested that teachers ask students to stipulate this by the use of qualifying words, such as: *it might be that*, or, perhaps, or *maybe*.

One of the important benefits of becoming habituated to suggesting hypotheses in facing a problem is that it becomes easier to avoid jumping to conclusions, to seeing only a single answer, a single rationale. In detective or police work, this is a crucial skill—as it is tempting to point blame at a potential culprit in order to quickly solve the mystery, rather than putting minds to work in examining evidence and suggesting alternate possibilities (e.g., hypotheses) as potential avenues of exploration.

But that arena is far from the only one in which the ability to see several options as possible avenues of exploration is important. For government officials in federal, state, civic, and international situations, it would be essential to use hypothesizing in dealing with the many and varied problems facing their constituencies. Teachers also use hypothesizing to make diagnoses of individual learning problems and their hypotheses often lead to several means of examining what is happening that gets in the way of a student's ability to learn.

It would be not only naive, but also irresponsible, to arrive at simplistic conclusions in any of these areas of professional functioning without first examining all the evidence available and suggesting potential avenues of exploration and eventual determination of cause and solution. It would not be an exaggeration to claim that acts of war have been waged when those in power have jumped to conclusions, without regard for evidence and without examining hypotheses to attempt to explain a potentially aggressive state of affairs.

A case in point is found the compelling book *Act of War* (2013) by Jack Cheevers, who writes about the seizing of the spy ship the *Pueblo*, by the North Koreans, providing details of how federal negotiators under the Lyndon Johnson administration worked to try to save the imprisoned sailors from execution and prevent the situation from escalating into war. The book describes how, by using many potential hypotheses as tools for their interventions and applying high-level intelligence and careful diplomacy, this served to free the men and prevent further confrontations with the North Koreans.

It cannot be overemphasized that students who become more skilled in using hypotheses in dealing with problems have essential tools in becoming habituated to the kind of thinking that involves seeing many alternatives in problem solving, thereby exercising more intelligent habits of mind.

Before undertaking any work in creating or choosing hypothesizing activities for students, teachers should be aware that an *a priori* condition should prevail. That is, the problems or dilemmas created or selected should be grounded in students' experiences, grade-level curriculum, or current events. If the problems chosen are too complex and too removed from students' experiences (e.g., what are some hypotheses that might explain why people resort to terrorism to address their grievances?), the result might end up as a guessing game, the responses too far removed from reality to make the activity worthwhile.

So the problems chosen should fall within the range of the students' experiences or studies before they move into more complex and far-reaching analyses. That is not to say that the problems chosen should be simplistic; but there is a big difference between what is trivial and what has meaning in students' studies and in their lives.

Once again, curriculum guides and subject areas should provide many rich areas of study from which hypothesizing activities can be extracted. Current issues in the news may also be a fruitful source for developing hypothesizing tasks. But as a starting point, teachers may want to consider some of the suggestions below.

CLASSROOM APPLICATIONS

Social studies, for example, is rife with possibilities for hypothesizing. However, other subject areas offer many options as well.

- Many early civilizations arose in river valleys. How do you account for that? What hypotheses can you suggest?
- How do you explain Cleopatra's influence on Caesar? How do you account for the fact that such a strong and powerful leader as Caesar would fall under Cleopatra's spell?
- How do you suppose that it was possible for the Romans to build such a great empire, from such humble beginnings? What explanations can you suggest?
- How do you explain the rise of such cultural achievements in the Roman Empire, as architecture, poetry, medicine, and theater? What hypotheses can you suggest?
- How do you explain the fall of this great Roman Empire? What hypotheses can you suggest?
- How do you suppose athletics serves as entertainment? What are your ideas about it?
- How do you see competition as an attractive feature of society? What hypotheses can you suggest to explain it?

- How did the ability to read and write contribute to early civilizations? What hypotheses can you suggest to explain it?
- Some powerful leaders demand great monuments to honor and immortalize them. What explains this? What hypotheses can you suggest?
- People living in large groups require rules and laws to govern their behavior. What hypotheses explain this need?
- People throughout history have had a deep fear of the unknown and of life's uncertainties. What hypotheses can you suggest that might explain this?
- People throughout history have made war in order to increase their status, their power, and their possessions. What hypotheses can you suggest how people might believe that war would help them do that?
- How do you explain the rise of strong fundamentalist views in the Muslim religion? What hypotheses can you suggest?
- What do you consider to be some significant sources of tension between the Palestinians and the Israelis? What hypotheses can you suggest that might explain it?
- How does frustration lead to violence? How do you explain it?
- What do you consider to be some reasons to explain the human dispersal across many continents during the Paleolithic age? What are your ideas?
- What in your view motivates people living in groups to violent behavior? What hypotheses can you suggest to explain it?
- How did the caste system in India serve the purposes of the government? What ideas do you have to explain it?
- How was it possible for England to take over the rule of India for nearly a hundred years? What hypotheses can you suggest to explain this phenomenon?
- How did the acceptance of slavery in the United States serve the economy? What are your hypotheses about that?
- What do you suppose makes it possible for some people to sanction the use of slavery? What hypotheses can you suggest?
- What do you suppose accounts for the attraction of men to have joined the Crusades—the religious wars between the Christians and Muslims that carried on for nearly 200 years? What hypotheses can you suggest to explain it?
- Women had few rights during the Middle Ages and behavior was strictly controlled by the church. What do you suppose explains that?
- What role do you suppose morale plays in obtaining support for a war? What hypotheses can you suggest?
- What do you suppose accounted for the incident called the Dust Bowl in the United States in the 1930s? What hypotheses can you suggest to explain it?
- What do you suppose accounted for the hostility toward the "Okies" as they migrated west during the Dust Bowl years? How do you explain it?

- What explains the US government's attempts to annihilate the First Nations tribes during the eighteenth and nineteenth centuries? What hypotheses can you suggest?
- What accounted for the rise of the Nazis to power in Germany in the early twentieth century? What explains it?
- What do you suppose explains people's beliefs in the supernatural? What hypotheses can you suggest?
- What explains some people's willingness to believe fake news? What hypotheses can you suggest?
- Why do you suppose politicians use "spin" to influence people's thinking? What hypotheses can you suggest to explain it?
- What explains the Bolsheviks' need to murder Czar Nicholas and his family as they rose to power during the Russian Revolution? What hypotheses can you suggest?
- What, in your view, underlies people's racist beliefs? What hypotheses can you suggest?
- What in your view explains the continued segregation of schools in the US south after the Civil War? What hypotheses can you suggest?

As well in other curriculum areas:

- What do you suppose explains the extinction of many animal species? What hypotheses can you suggest?
- How do you explain the influence of the moon on tides? What hypotheses can you suggest?
- What do you suppose are some concerns about genetically modified foods? What hypotheses can you suggest?
- How, in your view, is organic food better for our diets? What hypotheses can you suggest to explain it?
- How does our knowledge of DNA serve us? What hypotheses can you suggest to explain it?
- How do you explain the rise of obesity among young people in the United States? What hypotheses can you suggest?
- Why do you suppose the way people look is so important in making decision about them? What hypotheses can explain that?
- How did the discovery of wheels benefit civilizations? What hypotheses can you suggest to explain it?
- How does our skin "send messages to our brains"? What ideas do you have about how this works?
- How do our senses serve us? What hypotheses can you suggest?
- What is it about dogs that enables them to make such good pets? What hypotheses can you suggest to explain it?

- How come some measurements are inaccurate? How do you explain it?
- How come certain kinds of food left out of the fridge spoil after three days? How do you explain it?
- How come some people believe in UFOs? What hypotheses can you suggest to explain it?
- What are some reasons for space exploration? What hypotheses can you suggest to explain why this is a good thing to do?
- What do you suppose explains the opposition to the scientific evidence about global warming? What hypotheses can you suggest?
- What predictions can you make about the use of driverless cars? What hypotheses can you suggest that would explain what changes would be seen?
- How could you measure a balloon? What ideas do you have that would explain how this could be done?
- What would be some ways in which you could budget your allowance? What hypotheses can you suggest that would help you to do this?
- How come some students are bullies? How do you explain it?
- How could you figure out how many half cups of water it would take to fill a bathtub? Suggest some hypotheses for how you might figure this out.
- What would be some good ways to help bullies become nicer people? What hypotheses can you suggest as some plans?
- Why do you suppose how people look is important? How do you explain it?
- What accounts for the popularity of the Harry Potter books? How do you explain it?
- How come Twitter has become so important in people's lives? How do you explain it?
- What would happen if everyone gave up their cell phones for a day? What do you think?
- What do you suppose are the most important elements in a good book? What are your thoughts about it?
- What do you suppose makes Harry Potter an interesting character? What are your ideas about it?
- Where do people's prejudices come from? What hypotheses can you suggest to explain it?

The above are only a few suggestions to give teachers an idea of how some big ideas in the curriculum can be the basis for the development of hypothesizing activities. These tasks can be carried out individually, in small groups, or in a whole class discussion and there are benefits to any of those procedures. However, it is suggested that whichever way is chosen, follow-up questions should be raised that further engage student thinking and stimulate deeper inquiry. For example,

- How did you arrive at your hypotheses? Where did your ideas come from?
- Which ones on your list of hypotheses seem most credible to you? Which seem more reasonable as potential explanations? Why do you think that's true?
- Which of your hypotheses seems least credible? Which seems "out of the ball park" with respect to what is a good explanation? Why do you think that's true?
- What ideas do you have about testing your hypotheses?
- What data would you need to accept one hypothesis as more reasonable than others?

After such discussions, teachers may wish to ask students to revisit their responses and make any changes they believe are warranted by their further explorations. As well, it is always a good idea to ask students, in retrospect, how such an activity was helpful or of significance to their thinking. Such *post hoc* examinations serve to give voice to and provide rationale for the role of more intelligent thinking in their lives.

SCENES FROM THE CLASSROOM

The children sit quietly around the table with impeccably good manners. They are well groomed in their designer jeans and expensive haircuts. But their stylish appearance does not divert from the apprehension in their eyes. The teacher removes a card from a large box of thinking activities and offers it for their study.

"How do you suppose pigeons can be trained to deliver messages?"

They are clearly stumped and there is a long pregnant silence, after which Sharon timidly queries, "Could you tell us what you mean?"

The teacher repeats the question, unwilling to play into their transparent ruse of soliciting clues to "the answer." The repeated question again draws silence. Finally, Des mumbles, "We didn't study birds yet."

And

How do you suppose birds learn to fly?
Carol (age 5): I think it's natural insect.

Chapter 8

Introduction to Searching Out Assumptions

On the one hand, making assumptions helps us to wade through a lot of information and draw some conclusions. On the other hand, making unwarranted assumptions may cause us to infer data that are wrong, or absent—thereby putting us in positions of making decisions that have negative or unintended consequences.

For example, the salesperson on TV pitches a product that he claims to be "proven" as doing the job of getting the grease out of dirty dungarees. He has a handsome face, elegant clothes, and a $300 haircut. We are quickly persuaded that this "nice guy" is telling the truth and we assume that "proven" means that there is a guarantee that that detergent, will, in fact, dispatch ugly grease stains from trousers. However, we may be in for a disappointment.

A well-known TV personality advertises that the medicine that he takes makes him feel more energetic. Many people were persuaded by his claim, since, after all, he was a TV star. It was a scam. The medical clinic in Philadelphia advertises that it can cure cancers that other hospitals cannot cure. Should we make an assumption about the truth of its claim?

Assuming means taking for granted information beyond what is said, heard, read, seen, and even smelled—and if we choose not to examine those assumptions carefully and judiciously, we may be led down the garden path.

The NASA scientists assumed the rubber O-rings on the seals of the rocket ship would not alter under conditions of extreme cold. It was a bad assumption and the astronauts who were thrust into space were all killed when the spacecraft exploded. Richard Feynman, testifying before a congressional committee, demonstrated, by dipping an O-ring into a glass of ice water, that the rubber did indeed change shape by expanding, thus corrupting the seals. Taking assumptions as truths may have very serious negative consequences.

Not that assumptions, in and of themselves, are bad. We go about our business everyday making all kinds of assumptions. What is important is our ability to recognize that assumptions are not facts and that we need to be wary of them and suspend judgment—especially in incidents of relevance, or significance. If we draw conclusions based on faulty assumptions, we may be in for a lot of trouble.

Differentiating assumptions from facts, no matter how deeply our belief systems want to embrace them, is key to more intelligent thinking and more rational decision making. This is especially true today, when the internet makes us vulnerable to an avalanche of advertisements, enticing us to purchase things that are, on surface, appealing and cheap, but, in fact, may be coming from scammers from abroad, whose hacking into our systems is pervasive.

Even more important is our ability to search for assumptions in the presence of "news" that comes from the internet, social media, radio, and TV, which may not be news at all, but large doses of false information, deliberately designed to deceive. Learning to suspend judgment, to wait for confirming data, may be one of the most important tools that we can give our students so that they may respond rationally rather than with emotionality.

One of the ways in which unwarranted assumptions get us into trouble is with the kinds of attributions we make about others, based on their appearance, their skin color, their ethnic backgrounds, the neighborhoods in which they live, the kinds of food they eat, their manner of speech, and other such surface attributes. Drawing conclusions about others based on attributions about them is not only faulty, but also the underpinnings of prejudicial thinking. Learning to be wary about making unwarranted assumptions about others is an important way of building better human relationships.

It has been said that people these days are gullible, easy persuaded by shoddy propaganda, and lacking in critical acumen. It has also been said that such gullibility is part and parcel the result of a barrage of information, coming from all kinds of sources, in a continuous, endless stream, bombarding us with more information than we can possibly digest. The result is that we cherry-pick what "feels" more comfortable to us—news that fits in with our already established mind-sets. In that way, we are more vulnerable to assumptions that may lead us astray in making decisions of consequence.

A case in point is the incident in Twin Falls, Idaho (Dickerson 2017), where the townsfolk, by and large, were suckered, through false news feeds, into making more and more bizarre assumptions about what was believed to be an "assault of a minor child." The story escalated into wilder and wilder exaggerations, resulting in a town torn apart, with accusations rampant against minority citizens.

The news, op-ed articles, TV, tweets, and the internet, all the modern media, offer a substantial lode of material that begs to be examined more closely. If students spend more time in critically searching for and more mindful of assumptions, they are more likely to develop more discrimination, more discernment, and more resistance to propositions that are, on the surface, persuasive, but faulty. Without such discernment, and such intelligent discrimination, we may be tempted to believe that all people from Arab countries are terrorists, that all people of color are not to be trusted, that there is no such thing as global warming, that Darwin's theory is only a theory, and that vaccinations are harmful for children.

It is easy, as Kahneman (2011) points out, to fall back on System One thinking in defense of faulty data—and that is why the kind of analysis of information needed in intelligent examination of assumptions may be more important today than ever before in our history.

Looking for assumptions that are being made, and those that we are making in behalf of a certain point of view, is an enormously helpful exercise for students who are to become the future decision makers in a democratic society. Questions such as "Is that true?" and "How do you know it's true?" and "What data do you have that support that?" ask students to be more discriminating, more discerning, and more responsible consumers of information.

There are literally hundreds of ways in which students can be asked to search for assumptions within the standard curriculum frameworks of each grade. Of course, current events offer rich sources of material. A search for assumptions can begin with the identification of a problem—and both before the problem is tackled and again, after the solution is proposed, a search for assumptions can identify the areas in which students need to exercise caution in drawing conclusions and making decisions of consequence.

Some examples of suggested activities that cover several curriculum areas are offered below. This is a very small sample of how students can exercise higher-order thinking in searching out assumptions. Where data are being examined, students should also be encouraged to use a fact-check source from the internet to ascertain whether the data are accurate and rooted in fact.

One such site is www.factcheck.org, a project of the Annenberg Policy Center. Since so few students as well as adults make use of fact-checking sources, instead relying on what pops up first on their search engines (Wineberg and McGrew 2016) without regard to whether the information is accurate or not, this may be, for most of them, a new skill, which should be not only encouraged, but also given some specific "how to" directions.

CLASSROOM APPLICATIONS

- How can we determine what factors influence the weather? What assumptions are being made?
- How can we tell if the soil outside of the school would be good for planting a vegetable garden? What assumptions are being made in the proposals?

- What experiments can be set up to show that foods contain protein (starch, sugar)? What assumptions are being made in the proposal?
- If the class is going on a trip, how may we decide on the transportation? What time factors are involved? What money will be needed for the costs? What other arrangements need to be made? What assumptions are being made in each of these proposals?
- How can our class make a significant contribution to our school or neighborhood? What assumptions are being made in the proposal?
- How might we make our studies of other countries more real to us? What assumptions are being made in the proposal?
- How can we go about inviting a guest speaker to our class? What assumptions are being made in the proposal?
- What are some good ways to measure the capacity of a container? What assumptions are being made in the proposal?
- What is the best way to cut a pumpkin pie into seven equal pieces? What assumptions are being made in the proposal?
- What, in your view, contributes to the continuing racial discrimination in the United States? What assumptions are being made in your thinking?
- How did the Civil Rights Act help in the elimination of segregation? What assumptions are being made in your thinking?
- How successful was the Civil Rights Act in ending racial discrimination? What assumptions are being made in your responses?
- What explains the fall of Communism in the Soviet Union? What assumptions are being made in your responses?
- What explains the rise of Communism in the Soviet Union? What assumptions are being made in your responses?
- How would you describe the key events of the twentieth century? What assumptions are being made in your responses?
- What assumptions were being made when prisoners entering the Auschwitz concentration camp saw the sign, "Arbeit Macht Frei"? What are your ideas about it?
- What do you consider to be the major problems facing modern civilization in the next fifty years? What assumptions are being made in your responses?
- What role might an individual play in contributing to the healthful future of this planet? What assumptions are being made in your responses?
- How can a single person make a positive difference? What assumptions are being made in your responses?
- How did climatic conditions, geography, and supplies of food contribute to the development of civilizations in the Neolithic period? What assumptions are being made in your responses?
- How is it possible that a star football player earns ten times more money than a teacher? What are your ideas about it? What assumptions are being made in your responses?

- What kinds of jobs should be the highest paid? What assumptions are being made in your responses?
- Philip's father is thinking about buying a new car, one that no longer needs a driver. What assumptions might he be making?
- How should schools deal with bullies? What assumptions are being made in your responses?
- How does music benefit our lives? What assumptions are being made in your responses?
- How does art benefit our lives? What assumptions are being made in your responses?
- What makes "good" art? What assumptions are being made in your responses?
- What's "good" music? What assumptions are being made in your responses?
- What makes for a good story? What assumptions are being made in your responses?
- What might be some measures our city or town might take to help the homeless? What assumptions are being made in your proposals?
- What makes certain types of clothing more desirable than others? What are your ideas? What assumptions are being made in your responses?
- What makes cell phones so important in our lives? What are your ideas? What assumptions are being made in your responses?
- How come Sherlock Holmes continues to be such an interesting character after all these years? What are your thoughts about it? What assumptions are being made in your responses?

Another way to approach the examination of assumptions is through written statements in which students are asked to study the text and search for the ways in which assumptions have been made by the speaker or writer. For example,

(a) "He's so good looking. I think I'm going to vote for him for class president."
(b) "He asked me to lend him my autographed hockey card so that he could show it to his friends. I gave him my card and he lost it."
(c) The World War I soldier was suffering from "battle fatigue" and had lost his speech. The doctor said, "We will give him some electric shock treatments and that will shock him back to speech."
(d) "General Eisenhower was such a good soldier. He helped us win World War II. That is why I think he will make a good president."
(e) In the United States, women were not considered eligible to vote until 1920. Arguments against woman's suffrage included statements like "All government rests ultimately on force, to which women, owing to physical, moral and social reasons, are not capable of contributing."

(f) "If we allow immigration, the newcomers will take away jobs from those
      of us already here."
(g) "The reason for the American Revolution was taxes."
(h) "Living in the suburbs is better than cities. It's safer."
(i) "Men should earn more than women for the same jobs. They are stronger
      and work harder."

One more area in which a search for assumptions can be fruitful is in examining
the slogans offered in advertisements, in politics, in history, in health, in diet,
and in other current and historical sources that attempt to capture a message with
a brief label and win support for a particular "side." Many assumptions must be
made in interpreting the label, and it would not be surprising to discover that
different people interpret and assume different meanings and different values in
each. But the effects of all are the same—to drum up approval and to foment
support without having to think or consider the meanings behind the messages.

There are many instances in recent and older historical periods where
labels and slogans have "played to the gallery," stirred up emotions, and
incited followers to a particular cause. For example, consider:

- Luxury, you deserve it.
- Save money; live better.
- Save freedom of worship! Buy war bonds!
- It's smart to save.
- The sky's the limit.
- Guns don't kill. People do.
- Liberty and justice for all.
- Real men wear blazers.
- The secret of getting ahead is getting started.
- An eye for an eye.
- Ein volk, ein Reich, ein Fuhrer.
- Just do it!
- Eat your greens to fit into your jeans.
- An apple a day keeps the doctor away.
- Make my day.
- Whatever.

Fake news, coming from TV, the tabloid press, the internet, and social media,
cries out for the examination of assumptions. This is not only a fruitful area
for study, but also perhaps a critical one, which can be done through asking
students to bring in samples of what they have seen and heard and collected,
and putting them under critical examination in a class discussion.

In summary, we go through life-making assumptions, and while these are often easy ways to facilitate our decisions, what remains important is that they be recognized for what they are, remembering that assumptions are not truths but conjectures. And in making decisions of consequence, they need to be verified before they can claim to be valid indicators of what is. So while assumptions are not errors, it is the ability to identify statements as assumptions that is a necessary condition of higher-order thinking and improved ability to make informed decisions.

Once students have had some work in their searching for assumptions, it is helpful to engage them in a whole class discussion, using higher-order questions that tap into their thinking and help them achieve greater awareness of where they are on solid ground in their views and where the ice is thin and they are in danger of falling through.

Questions may be such as the following:

- What makes you think that is true? What data do you have to support that idea?
- Where is your information coming from? What sources do you consider to be valid?
- "Billy" doesn't share your opinion. How can we decide who is right?
- Can you give me an example of how that can work?
- Why is that important to you?
- How do you know that is true?
- If that is true, what do you see as some consequences?

Being respectful in hearing students' ideas, however they seem to be "off the wall," is a *sine qua non* in furthering their thinking and allowing them to develop as intelligent consumers of data.

SCENES FROM THE CLASSROOM

The teacher gave her fourth-grade students a math problem in which the farmer had a bucket of eggs. She said, "The farmer reached his hand into the bucket five times and each time pulled out 3 eggs. How many eggs were in the bucket?"

Paula raised her hand and said, "You can't tell, because you don't know how many eggs were in there in the first place. There could be more eggs left in the bucket."

And the teacher responded: "Don't be such a smart aleck. Just answer the question."

Chapter 9

Introduction to Summarizing

It takes a bit of mental work to look at a lengthy piece of information and extract the important ideas, to distill out the essence. The task requires the ability to differentiate between what are the essentials and what are the more minor aspects of the whole message. To do this requires a considerable amount of mental effort, exercising the brain.

There is no single way of summarizing and different students may find different "essentials" in one piece of writing, or in one experience, or in one story, or in one news article, or in one internet posting. While there may be minor disagreements about the essentials, what is important is that students learn to differentiate between the important ideas and those that are of less relevance. When students can do this, they gain greater awareness of what is relevant, what is of less consequence, and what is of great and of lesser significance.

These skills contribute to the development of greater discrimination. This is not an easy operation and some students may require some practice in learning to summarize effectively. But practice in summarizing, in distilling from the whole what the key elements are, will lead to better habits of thinking and more intelligent discrimination of what is essential and what is of less consequence. Summarizing also becomes a way of differentiating between what is factual and what are "laid on" embellishments that have little or no significance to the core issues.

Looking at the way newspapers write headlines to encapsulate lengthy news articles may give students first-level experiences in understanding how summaries are made as well as examining how accurately they represent or misrepresent the news. Students may be asked to create their own headlines and to write summaries of films, of stories, a class trip, a visit to a museum, a political address, a candidate's platform, a TV program, a superhero's attributes, and a school program. The ways in which students can be asked to summarize are legion.

The importance of being able to summarize intelligently can be developed via many different kinds of curriculum tasks. Once again, what's important in summarizing is to develop those skills that enable the extraction of meaning, to the exclusion of what is irrelevant, insubstantial, or blatantly false.

The standard curriculum offers many opportunities for students to engage in summarizing activities—and while the examples offered below are suggestions, they may serve to point teachers to the how and the what of summarizing tasks. Teachers will be the best judges of which are more appropriate for their students based on their levels of maturity and sophistication, as well as their previous experiences in summarizing.

CLASSROOM APPLICATIONS

To initiate students into the operation of summarizing, first steps may include *titling*, or *captioning* newspaper articles, stories, black-and-white photos, cartoons, poems, graphs, and chapters in textbooks. They may also examine headlines in newspapers and compare the way the headlines accurately summarize the news article.

What follows are a few dozen more sophisticated suggestions about what kinds of summaries can be made.

- The first voyage of Columbus from Genoa to the Americas
- The voyage of the Beagle, a narrative of Charles Darwin's journey from Plymouth Sound to the South Pacific
- The story of Moby Dick
- The life of the artist Vincent van Gogh
- The biographical history of the first black president of the United States, Barack Obama
- The assassination of John F. Kennedy
- The history of slavery in the United States
- The critical battles of the Civil War
- The presidency of Abraham Lincoln
- The decline of the Roman Empire
- Any of the Harry Potter books
- The steps leading up to the Boston Tea Party
- The critical incidents in "Ten Days That Shook the World"
- The steps leading to the rise of National Socialism in Germany
- The stages in the life cycle of the butterfly

- The events leading up to and subsequent to the Dust Bowl in the United States in the 1930s
- The events leading up to the Great Depression that began in 1929
- The process of turning metal into steel
- The process of turning crude oil into gasoline
- The history of the automobile
- The history of the airplane
- The development of the first computer
- A biography of Nikola Tesla
- The role of Alan Turing in decoding Nazi communications in World War II
- The history of space travel in the United States
- The history of the electric car
- How milk becomes butter
- The life cycle of salmon
- The rise of the use of cellphones
- The history of the development of numbers
- Archimedes physical law of buoyancy
- The life of Mozart
- The caste system in India
- The story of the Crusades
- Lives of women in the Middle Ages
- The factors that brought down the feudal system of land control in the Middle Ages
- The life of Ignaz Semmelweis
- The history of the significance of antisepsis in medical practice
- The significance of the Renaissance for modern art and architecture
- The history of repression of thinking in the Middle Ages
- The key principles of a totalitarian government
- The influence of the printing press on the quality of lives and thinking during the middle of the fifteenth century
- The steps leading up to Brexit
- The impact of colonialism in selected African countries
- The role of the Swiss during World War II
- The role of NAFTA in promoting trade in North America
- The effects of global warming on the Arctic
- The events leading up to and subsequent to the Industrial Revolution
- The events leading up to and subsequent to the IT revolution
- The events leading up to and subsequent to the Triangle Factory fire
- The settlement of the west in the United States and its impact on Native Americans
- The significant advances in technology in the late twentieth and early twenty-first centuries

- The impact of immigration on North American cultures in the early twentieth century
- The impact of immigration in Europe in the late twentieth and early twenty-first centuries
- Some specific instances that reveal ingrained prejudice toward the lives of black Americans
- The appeal of fascism in Italy and Germany in the twentieth century
- The events leading up to and subsequent to the Holocaust
- A summary of the history of the Civil Rights movement in the United States
- The steps involved in division of fractions
- The Pythagorean theorem
- How to train a dog to fetch a newspaper
- The Monroe Doctrine
- The Underground Railroad
- The rules for Nintendo Gameboy
- The uncertainty principle
- The Copernican theory

The examples above offer only a very brief set of examples of what is possible in asking students to exercise their minds in creating summaries of important events. What is important, however, is ensuring that students have many varied and rich opportunities to summarize, thus exercising their abilities to condense the key ingredients of larger pieces of information and distilling from them what is essential, what is important, what is factual, and what are distortions of fact.

Of course, it is a given when students are asked to summarize these events, they begin with a body of data. Working from written or visual material is much more productive than asking them to retrieve events from memory, which at best can be fragmented, spotty, or, worse, full of inaccuracies.

Many teachers who have been using "teaching for thinking" curriculum frameworks suggest that when students have opportunities to work together, in teams of two or three on these tasks, there is much to be gained from that interchange of ideas. As students "play out" their ideas from one to the other, the result is often richer, with more varied perspectives. As well, when a single student's idea is muddled, or wrong-headed, the other members of the study group have a chance to weigh in and offer alternative points of view. All of this increases and enriches understanding and depth of thinking and pays off richly in the whole class discussion in which all students' ideas are shared.

When summaries have been completed, it is a good idea for students to compare their work with each other, and in this way, gain new perspectives on the essentials as well determining which, of many different summaries, is the most viable in identifying "what's important." The teacher's responses in this "debriefing" promote further thought through the use of higher-order questions, such as the following:

- How did you figure out that those elements were the most important?
- Which parts of the whole did you consider leaving out? What made you consider those to be of less importance?
- How did you determine the accuracy of the information? How did you determine what was inaccurate or false?
- When two students have different views of the important and key elements in their summaries, how do we figure out which more accurately represents the important issues? What are your thoughts about that?
- Why do you suppose the ability to summarize is important? What thoughts do you have about it?

Once the discussion has concluded and ideas have been reexamined, the students may be asked to return to their summary statements and make any changes they consider important. This "revisiting" of their summaries gives them another chance to reflect, and to reexamine what's key, what's important, what's blatantly false, and what may be safely omitted without losing the essential elements of the whole.

SCENES FROM THE CLASSROOM

Mark, a fifth grader, made a summary of his autobiography:

When I grow up I would like to be like Albert Einstein. One reason is that he is a great celebrity. Oh, I know there are many more celebrities in the world but none as smart as him. I would make a lot of money and many jobs would be open to me. There are a lot of reasons but I am just an average boy who has to finish his lunch in a candy store.

Chapter 10

Introduction to Interpreting

A group of four people were coming out of the theater, and they were talking together about the "meaning" of the play *China Doll* they had just seen. Judy said, "Now what was that all about? I couldn't figure it out."

Stanley offered, "I think it's about a very rich man who has just bought an airplane for his young fiancée."

Judy responded, "Oh I think there has to be more to it than that. I think it's about the relationship between the older man and his assistant."

Gilda shook her head. "No, I don't think that's the main message of the play. I think it's about whether having a lot of money gets you what you really want in your life."

Mel countered, "No, I don't agree. I think the airplane is a metaphor. I think it stands for being able to get whatever you want if you only had the money."

Listening to them, it was clear that they took different meanings from the drama. The interpretations of what they had seen seemed to be representative of different perspectives, different experiences. Some experiences are open to wider interpretations, some of which are more viable than others. Some experiences are more restrictive in the kinds of interpretations that may be made from the body of data. In the former cases, the data are more "soft," coming from written work such as essays, novels, plays, and poetry. In the latter cases, the data are "hard" and come from graphs, charts, photographs, and maps. In either case, the task calls for reading meaning into, or taking meaning out of the data.

It is perhaps one of the more difficult of the thinking operations, since there is such a great tendency for not only children but adults as well not only to generalize on the basis of insufficient evidence, but also to "read in" to an experience what is not actually there. The big danger in interpreting what is seen and read is filtering that data through one's own perceptual lens. We see what we want to see, not necessarily what is there.

So looking at the election of a particular candidate for office, one can "interpret" meaning and conclude, "The people want a change." This is hardly borne out by any data, because the reasons for the election of that candidate may be quite different as well as varying from population to population. Summing up the totality of the result in a simple "interpretation" is not only a leap beyond the data, but also a simplistic kind of thinking. Yet, many children and adults fall easily into that kind of trap. In such misinterpretations lies one root of misinformation. Or as one wag put it, "There are lies, damn lies and statistics."

There are also tendencies to go beyond the data in attributing cause, validity, and representativeness when these qualities are absent or in doubt. Sometimes extrapolations go far beyond what the data can support and despite that, they are offered with such conviction that it is difficult to counter with rational argument. It is not uncommon, for example, to find graduate students who have gathered data for their doctoral theses, trying to make sense of what the data are revealing and having great difficulty in freeing their minds from preconceived judgments about what they hoped the data would reveal, rather than acknowledging the more accurate interpretations of the facts.

Since belief systems are notoriously unyielding to fact, even at the graduate student level, "confirmation bias" (Mercier and Sperber 2017) creeps in as one wants to believe what is consistent with already held beliefs. In other words, emotionality trumps rational thinking more than we are likely to admit. And this tendency is most evident in exercises where interpreting data is the task.

In cases where the data are incomplete, or dubious, students' interpretations will need qualification. Qualifying words such as *probably*, or, perhaps, *or it seems*, can be used when the data are not clear and/or the inference is not on solid ground. Sometimes, inferences are more certain and this allows the language used to convey this degree of conviction. At other times, there is little clear-cut meaning that can be ascribed to or drawn from an experience. In such cases, it is important to indicate that the data are too vague, or too limited, to draw a sound interpretation.

Why would the ability to make sound and wise interpretations of data be an important skill in a world where misinformation is coming at us from many and varied sources, including TV "news," tabloid newspapers, and the internet, as well as our peers? The answer is obvious: if good information is one solid basis for intelligent and wise decision making, the ability to interpret that information allows us to become wiser, more informed, and more rational in how we think, and in how we behave. Learning how to make "good sense" from our experiences is a critical and valuable building block along the road to maturity.

It would not be an exaggeration to claim that interpreting what we see and hear is something we do a lot of in our daily lives, but perhaps we are not so much aware that we are interpreting. For example, we encounter a man poorly dressed walking across the street and interpret that he is a derelict, based only on his clothing. We hear a baby cry and interpret that the child is "cranky." A student fails to get her work finished on time and we attribute that "she is lazy." Parents fail to attend a parent-teacher conference and we interpret that they are unconcerned. A boy has trouble with his math problems and we interpret that he "didn't pay attention."

It's not hard to build a scenario to fill in the blanks when data are absent, where what is "filled in" confirms one's assumptions or set of beliefs. This is the case when those in charge are predetermined to see a person as guilty, and create their own biased scenarios to confirm those beliefs, with the ugly tendency to disregard any other data that do not fit into the belief system. We make these interpretations easily and often glibly, without digging deeper to gather more data to make our interpretations more accurate and more representative of what actually "is."

There are big prices to pay for such misinterpretations. The man across the street may be far from a derelict, only choosing to wear disreputable clothing because he doesn't care what he looks like. There may be several other reasons to explain why a baby cries, one of which may have to do with needing a diaper change. The student who doesn't get her work finished on time may be tired and worried because she has been kept awake by arguing parents. The parents who fail to attend the conference may both be working hard to put food on the table. The person considered "guilty" may be guilty only of being on the wrong side of the charge person's beliefs system.

We need much more data before we can safely interpret behavior; and we are on dangerous ground when we fail to see that our interpretations are only weak-minded guesses and do not take into full account the whole of the story. It cannot be overemphasized that misinterpretations can not only get us into a lot of trouble, but also make for a lot of mischief, bad decisions, inappropriate human interactions, and a dangerous tendency to believe what is false.

An egregious example of "don't confuse me with the data; my mind is made up" occurred when those in power positions in the government ignored the data that showed no weapons of mass destruction, and clung to previously held belief positions, prompting the US invasion of Iraq in 2003, beginning the second Gulf War.

An important caveat in assigning students interpreting activities is to avoid what is trivial or inconsequential and engaging them in activities that can bring more important meanings to their understanding of what makes the world work. In that regard, some examples of interpreting data activities are offered below. But once again, teachers will find, within their curriculum guides, and content areas, issues of substance that can be the source of many rich opportunities to interpret, giving students not only practice in the thinking operation, but also bringing richer and deeper understanding to their lives.

Students who have a tendency to generalize on the basis of insufficient evidence—going far beyond what the data allow in drawing conclusions—give evidence that they are not yet equipped to operate at this higher level of thinking and that more, much more, experience with this skill is needed.

CLASSROOM APPLICATIONS

Interpreting activities, for novices, can begin with simple graphs, or charts, cartoons, and photographs. More sophisticated interpreting experiences can be based on work from history and the social studies, economics, science, political science, and literature. One needn't stray from the required curriculum to find and generate opportunities for students to engage in data interpretation. Some examples are offered below, and teachers who are choosing from them are cautioned to begin with less sophisticated tasks and work toward more challenging materials.

Activities for beginning work in Interpreting may include such tasks as calling for students' determinations of whether statements are true, false, or have insufficient data to make those determinations. Here are several examples:

- Read the following article and try to determine if the statement below is True (T), False (F), or if there is insufficient evidence to support the statement as true or false (I).

A software program designed for children who are having trouble with reading has been proved to be so successful in Surrey schools that the district has been moved to purchase the program for all schools in the district. The program is not only about reading. It is designed to change the way students process the smallest units of sound. Through the use of computer exercises, students of all ages can be exposed to sounds within sounds that are drawn out until they are able to distinguish them separately and, later, understand how they fit together into phonemes, the building blocks of all languages. The sounds are presented as a game, with rewards for correct answers and advancement based on results.

    (a)   This new program has been proven to be successful with children who have difficulty with reading.
    (b)   The students get a reward if they get a correct answer.
    (c)   The school district is enthusiastic about the results.
    (d)   Every district should buy this program.

(e) The program is good only for young children.
(f) It's very difficult to learn to use this program.
(g) The program was designed by teachers.
(h) It's important for students to learn how to read.
(i) The program is successful because it is like playing a game.
(j) Technology is a big help for students who have learning problems.

- Table 10.1 shows average salaries for people in different professions. Study the table and decide if the statements below are true, false, or whether there is insufficient information to decide if the statement is true or false (I), based upon the data in the table.

Table 10.1 Average Salaries of Professionals in the United States

Occupation	Average Salary per Year
Private First Class Seaman in the US Navy	$18,000
President of the United States	$400,000
Average Teacher	$44,683
Tom Brady (NFL Star)	$14,800,000
Surgeon	$225,000
Katy Perry (Pop Star)	$135,000,000
Police Officers (Average)	$44,255

(a) Police officers, on average, earn less than surgeons.
(b) Private First Class seamen earn more than teachers.
(c) Teachers are more important than football stars.
(d) You can figure out how much an average teacher earns in a month.
(e) How much a person earns is an indicator of his or her value to society.
(f) Katy Perry is a very good singer.
(g) Police officers should get a higher salary because they do a dangerous job.
(h) This table tells how much different professions earn in the United States.
(i) People choose their profession based on the salary they could earn.
(j) No singer is worth $135,000,000.

- Read the paragraph below and then try to decide whether the statements that follow are true, false, or whether there is insufficient data to make that determination, based on the information in the paragraph.

Iceland is a volcanic island in the North Atlantic Ocean. It was settled in the ninth century AD by Vikings, who established Europe's oldest constitutional government, in 930 AD. Christianity was introduced around 1000 AD. In the thirteenth century, Iceland acknowledged Norwegian rule. In the year 1380, Denmark conquered Iceland. Iceland gained its independence in 1918, but shared a king with the Danes. During World War II, first British and then

Chapter 10

American troops garrisoned the island. In 1944, when Denmark occupied by the Nazis, Iceland deposed its king and proclaimed itself a republic.

(a) Iceland is an island in the North Sea.
(b) The Vikings contributed substantially to the current Icelandic culture.
(c) Danish is the language of Iceland.
(d) The main religion of Iceland is Christianity.
(e) Iceland shares its king with the Danes.
(f)   During World War II, Iceland was occupied by Allied troops who were stationed there.
(g) A republic means that there is no king to rule the country.
(h) The Vikings came from Norway.
(i)   The population is small because it is so cold there.

• What statements can you make that are demonstrably true about the data in Table 10.2?

Table 10.2

NOBEL PRIZES: 1930–1956

	Physics	Chemistry	Medicine	Literature	Peace
United States	13	10	20	5	7
Germany	2	10	5	0	1
England	8	3	6	4	4
France	0	2	0	5	2
Sweden	0	1	1	2	1
Switzerland	0	2	3	1	0
Austria	3	0	1	1	0
Denmark	0	0	1	1	0
Holland	1	0	0	0	0
Italy	1	0	0	0	1
Belgium	0	0	1	0	0
Norway	0	0	0	0	0
Spain	0	0	0	0	0
Canada	0	1	0	0	0
Russia	0	1	0	0	0
Poland	0	0	0	0	0
India	1	0	0	0	0
Argentina	0	0	1	0	1
Finland	0	1	0	1	0
Chile	0	0	0	2	0
Hungary	1	0	1	0	0
Ireland	1	0	0	0	0
Japan	1	0	0	0	0
Iceland	0	0	0	1	0
Portugal	0	0	0	1	0
Puerto Rico	0	0	0	1	0

- Cartoons, photos, and other illustrations are good examples of what students can interpret, keeping in mind that they need to be on top of what is observably true, what is false, and what cannot be inferred from what is seen.
- Maps and graphs may also be used as exercises in interpreting the data that are found in these graphics.
- What interpretation do you put on the term "patriotism"? How do you see the term being used to arouse public response to a candidate's viability to elected office?
- As you read Tuchman's article "How We Entered World War I," how do you interpret the events that led to the beginning of hostilities that left 37,000,000 soldiers and civilians dead?
- From your reading of the text, what do you see as the economic and technological conditions that contributed to the emerging emancipation of women in the 1920s?
- From your reading of the text, what do you see as President Roosevelt's platform to deal with the economic crises of the Great Depression?
- From your viewing of the film *Come to the Paradise*, what do you see as the key factors that led to the internment of Japanese citizens on the West Coast during World War II?
- How do you explain the differences in treatment of German Americans and Japanese Americans in the United States and Canada during World War II? What data are you using to support your views?
- Many people experience times of war as times of great patriotic fervor, great national spirit, and great human purposefulness toward a common goal or cause. In retrospect, many people in Great Britain think back about the time of the London Blitz, when destruction of lives and property was extensive, with great nostalgia. How do you explain that?
- How do you explain Canada's "closed door" policy to Jewish refugees during World War II? What data support your view?
- Based on your viewing of the film *Broadcast News*, what do you see as the important messages in this film? What data from the film and from your supplementary reading support the film's position?
- Based on your viewing of the film *Wag the Dog*, what do you see as the important messages in this film? What data from the film and from your supplementary reading support the film's message?
- What is your interpretation of the term "medical ethics"? What data are you using in making that interpretation?
- What is your interpretation of the bumper sticker "A woman's place is in the mall"?

For Younger Children

- Observing how certain tools work (e.g., a shovel, a hammer, a saw, an egg beater, a pair of scissors, a stapler, a thermometer, a flashlight, an eraser, an air pump, a magnet) and making some statements about what is observably true in the operation of these tools.

- Live animal study—especially if there are pets in the classroom, for example, hamster, white mice, rabbit, snake, lizard, and gerbil—observing the animal over a period of time and making some observably true statements about what is seen, differentiating between what is true and what statements go beyond the data.
- Watching a film or a YouTube video of an egg hatching—and generating observably true statements about what is seen, differentiating between what is true and what statements go beyond the data.
- Studying photos of animals, such as whales, giraffes, tigers, and snakes—and asking students to make some statements that are observably true about what is seen, differentiating those that go beyond the data.
- Reading or listening to a story read—and making some observably true statements about what is read or heard, differentiating those that are observably true and those that go beyond the data.
- Dissecting an orange and making some observations about what is observably true and those statements that go beyond the data.
- Studying TV commercials, for example, ask students to make some statements about the products being advertised that are observably true and those that are patently false. Statements that go beyond the data should be identified and examined—noting particularly how advertising promotes such unwarranted assumptions.
- Studying racism, through photographs, for example, Norman Rockwell's illustration of Ruby Bridges being accompanied to school on the first day of desegregation in the South, along with the short paragraph about the illustration (see, e.g., http://en.wikipedia.org/wiki/File: The Problem_we_all_live_with_norman_rockwell.jpg)

This is an artist's painting of a real event that occurred in Louisiana, on November 14, 1960. Ruby Bridges is five years old. She is going to her first day in kindergarten. But she has to have four federal marshals walk with her—for fear of her life. That is because in New Orleans, this is the first day that Black children were allowed to enter what had been all-white schools, the first day of desegregation of schools in the South.

What statements can be made that are observably true about the photograph and the paragraph? What statements can be made that are observably false? Statements that go beyond the data should be identified and examined.

- Read the paragraph below and look at the statements that follow it. If a statement is true, mark it with a T. If a statement is clearly false, mark it with an F. If there is no evidence in the paragraph to support the statement, mark it with an I, for "insufficient data."

Cell phones have become essential tools in our lives. Some people think it is impossible to go out of the house without their cell phones. They make communication easy. Students use cell phones all the time and most of them go to school with their cell phones. Cell phones are not bad or harmful, but the problem is that some students use them for the wrong reasons and this makes for problems at school. Since most cell phones now can access the internet, students may use them to entertain themselves while they are supposed to be listening to the teacher. Not only is this a distraction, but it can also affect students' grades.

(a)   Cell phones are important in our lives.
(b)   They make being in communication simpler for us.
(c)   Some cell phones are harmful.
(d)   Teachers don't want you to bring cell phones to school.
(e)   Some students take cell phones to school for the wrong reasons.
(f)   Schools should outlaw cell phones in classrooms.
(g)   Cell phones are OK if you don't use them to access the internet.
(h)   Before we had cell phones, we needed to use the landlines at home.
(i)   Cell phones are too expensive for most students to buy on their own.

• Read the article below and make some statements about it that are demonstrably true and some that are clearly false.

It was easy for people to believe in witchcraft in the Middle Ages in Europe. Without any knowledge of science, people attributed abnormal events, like storms, drought, and plague, to the influence of Satan. And Satan was everywhere—and greatly feared. It was old women, who were, by and large, wrinkled and ugly and, therefore, especially vulnerable, who were considered to be influenced by Satan. For people who had no background in science, any strange or abnormal event could be claimed as witchcraft. Ignorant people believed that if the communities rid themselves of witches, things would return to normal.

Witches who "confessed freely" were sent to prison. Those who confessed under torture were given an "easy" death, by hanging or beheading.

Witch hunts made their way from Europe to Salem, Massachusetts, in 1692–1693. Nineteen people were tried and hanged, and one of them was pressed to death for refusing to testify. Five others, including two infant children, died in prison. The evidence of witchery came about in the dreams of the accused—which made defense impossible. Any dream could be taken as evidence that the accused was guilty. The Salem Witch Trials are considered to be one of the most notorious cases of mass hysteria, "an example of the dangers of religious extremism, false accusations, and failed due process."

It took twenty years for the courts of Salem to recant their errors and ask forgiveness of the families of those put to death.

- Using photos or a diagram of the life cycle of a plant, ask students to make some statements that are observably true and those that are demonstrably false, based on the data in the images.
- Ask the students to read the paragraph below and make some statements that are observably true and some that are demonstrably false, based on the evidence in the paragraph.

Most diseases are caused by microbes that invade the body. A more familiar term for these microbes is "germs."

Germs can enter the body through the air we breathe, through eating food or drinking water, through breaks in the skin, or through the bite of a carrier.

When we understand more about how germs are spread, it helps us to prevent disease.

The above examples offer some suggestions of the kinds of activities that can be used and/or developed to promote students' skills as intelligent interpreters of data. Through experience with these kinds of activities, students become more tuned in to what is observably true, what is patently false, and what assumptions are being made in the absence of verifiable data, thus making them more discriminating consumers of what is being presented in the media.

In selecting activities for classroom use, the teacher is always the best judge of which are more appropriate for his or her students, in terms of their age levels and their levels of maturity as well as their in-class and out-of-class experiences. While the above are examples of what can be done, teachers will find many ways to use their curriculum guides and textbooks to develop their own interpreting exercises for their students, thus giving them not only the "meat and potatoes" of the curriculum but also the ways of making the best and most intelligent understanding of what they are learning.

In classroom discussions that provide opportunities for students to reflect on their interpretations, the teacher's use of questions that engage further thought is more productive than the offering of rewards for good answers or admonitions for errors. For example,

- Can you tell me what data you are using to support that idea?
- Johann disagrees with your interpretation. Can you two tell me how you see those differences emerging?
- How do you see your own beliefs influencing your interpretations?
- Tell me more about what those data are telling you.
- Are you confident that you've thought this through?

Developing skill in the higher-order mental operation of Interpreting enables students to derive fuller meanings in their lives, adding to their abilities as rational decision makers. Students who have repeated and continued difficulty with interpreting and continue to "miss the meaning" are severely handicapped in their ability to make thoughtful, wise, informed, and intelligent decisions that may engender consequences that are unexpected, unforeseen, and even harmful.

SCENES FROM THE CLASSROOM

In the grade 6 classroom in which "teaching for thinking" was a key element of curriculum and instruction, the students were, to their frustration, rarely given advice or direction when they came to the teacher with questions or problems that the teacher thought they might be able to solve on their own. This, at first, met with students' frustration, and reproach (e.g., "What's the matter? Don't you know how to do it either?") but after time, the students grew in their ability to address and solve problems that arose with respect to assignments, and/or interpersonal problems on their own.

So when Eddie S. and Eddie M. came to him and asked him for specific help, they looked at him and said to each other, "He's never going to tell us anyway so we might as well go back and figure it out for ourselves."

Chapter 11

Introduction to Making Decisions

One of the most constant and pervasive mental activities in which adults engage in nearly every waking minute of their lives is decision making. From early morning, we are choosing—what to wear, what to have for breakfast (or not), whether we have time to scan the daily paper, and what plans to make for lunch. These nonessential decisions do not occupy a lot of mental space, and we generally do not give time or a lot of thought to making them. More critical choices face adults as they move through the day, choices that require more thoughtful consideration and often lead to consequences that affect their lives in the long or short term.

Decisions that have more significance require that we weigh the positive and negative aspects of the choice, and the emotional pulls that shift our thinking and lead us in one direction or another. "Bad" or "wrong" decisions may have dire consequences, but they also offer opportunities to reflect on how and why those choices were made and how we came about believing that those actions were "the right thing to do." So in some sense, we learn something from "bad" choices, but not without a price to be paid.

A free society requires and demands that choices be made with respect to our lived experiences as adults. In fact, this is what we expect and demand of a free society—an attribute that we prize and hold dear. We choose our educational pathways, our professions, our partners, our friends, our business associates, and our jobs. We choose candidates for office and we vote our choices; we choose the newspapers we read and the articles that inform our thinking; we choose the kinds of news programs we watch on TV and the commentators we think give us the best information. We choose the books we read, the magazines we subscribe to, and the recreational activities we engage in. We choose how we spend our hard-earned salaries, if we can afford a summer holiday, and, if so, where we will go.

Children, even at a young age, also engage actively in choosing and are often given opportunities to make their own choices. In fact, much has been written about the relationship between allowing children their choices and the development of their sense of personal power—for allowing children their choices communicates to them that we believe in them and in their ability to decide for themselves.

When children are given options, when they are allowed to choose, and when their choices are respected, they grow to believe in themselves; they learn that they "can do" (Glasser 1985). Allowing children choices empowers them. When their choices are delimited or circumscribed, they feel short-changed. It is part of our emotional needs makeup that we wish to choose for ourselves; that being denied our choices not only constrains, but also diminishes us.

Yet, learning to choose wisely—this essential tool of the mind—is rarely given a lot of attention in public education, where most of the important choices for students lie in the domain of teachers and administrators. With such proscriptions on students' decision making, how do they learn to make wiser, more intelligent choices in those things that matter most? How do they learn to study alternatives, weigh positive and negative aspects, and reflect on the consequences of their choices without adequate experience with such tasks? How can they learn about choosing wisely?

What if it might be possible for teachers to give students more opportunities to choose—to examine alternatives, to consider positive and negative aspects of the choice, to examine potential consequences, and to look at the beliefs, attitudes, and feelings that lie behind their choices—to decide "what's important"—so that they may learn to become more cognitively aware of how to make better and wiser choices? So that they become more aware of the ways in which emotions subvert conscious decision making? Could this be done within the confines of a school day, within the constraints of the prescribed curriculum?

"But I do that all the time," Ms. Bonniface claimed, when graduate student Gift (1989) asked to spend time in her classroom, observing the times and events in which decision making was given to students. Like the other teachers Gift observed, there was more belief in this teacher's thinking that her students did, in fact, have a lot of opportunities to choose, than Gift was able to see in actual classroom practice. Classroom activities that encouraged choosing and allowing students to reflect on their choices were not found in any abundance at any level of schooling (Gift 1989). When decisions are left to the students, it is usually in areas that do not truly matter. Shall you choose a red crayon or a blue one to color your wagon is of such little consequence that it reduces the act of choosing to banality.

It is not easy for teachers to give over decision-making responsibilities to their students primarily because such acts have historically been the prerogative of teachers. In some few instances, there are teachers who believe that allowing students to decide for themselves would corrupt the smooth running of a classroom. However, those teachers who have provided many and frequent opportunities for students to exercise their decision-making prerogatives will attest to the fact that students can and do rise to the occasion and often, with surprising wisdom and canny.

In those situations where choice has some relevance, in matters that truly count, students can be offered options, and examine the potential consequences of their actions, to themselves and others. They can become more alert to the ways in which emotions play a role in torqueing rational choices. This can be done more easily through presenting them with topics or issues about which they can reflect on "what's important" and where they would stand on such issues. "Pencil-and-paper" tasks would be one way of such explorations and examinations. Open-class discussions would be another.

When the topics and/or issues are related to the grade-level curriculum, this would make such discussions and examinations more relevant. And having made those choices, in the presence of higher-order questions that invite them to explore and examine (rather than in judgment), students have an opportunity to learn a little more about themselves—what kinds of people they are and what they stand for. Such practice enables them to grow in maturity and opens their minds to what they believe is right and what they believe is wrong, what they care deeply about and what is unimportant to them, and what they prize and what they scorn.

Such kinds of practice in decision making help students to learn to see both the assumptions they have made and consequences of their decisions and actions and to accept responsibility for them. These experiences promote an increased sense of responsibility, of personal agency, and lead toward maturity and more responsible adulthood.

When decision making is informed through reflection-on-action, our choices become wiser, more rational, more responsible, and we are less apt to fall for the slick and persuasive "snake oil" salespeople who want to sell us the emperor's new clothes. We are less susceptible to red herrings, to slogans, and to the rabble of the crowd.

If teachers see these goals as important in the education of their students, then they will be much more likely to provide them with many and diverse opportunities to engage them in activities in which they can choose where they stand, how they stand on certain issues, what emotional tugs pull at their conscious choices, and, in the end, come to a better realization of what is really important to them.

CLASSROOM APPLICATIONS

There exist classrooms in which students, at all levels, are offered choices in matters of curriculum. They may choose the books they want to read. They may choose projects that demonstrate their competence in certain curriculum areas. They may choose classmates with whom they wish to work with in group studies. In some classes, where personalized learning is prized and carried out, students have choices about not only subject matter, but also the amount of time they wish to spend on certain subjects and the amount of work they want to put into certain studies.

These may seem more radical ideas and may be off putting to some teachers. If that be the case, a more traditional way—with "pencil-and-paper" tasks or open classroom discussions—is also of value.

There are many topics for these kinds of activities and open classroom discussions that elicit "value-type" decisions about events, issues, people, situations, and the like. Students' statements would then be put under critical scrutiny, through the teacher's use of higher-order questions, such as the following:

- Can you give me an example of what you see as some potential consequences of that choice?
- Can you define what you mean by that?
- What are some alternatives you have considered?
- Where did your ideas come from?
- Are you confident that you have thought that through?
- Are there some assumptions that are being made here?
- If you did that, what do you see as some positive consequences of your choices?
- What do you see as some negative consequences?
- Are there some strong feelings you have that have influenced your thinking?
- Is this something you would advocate for others?
- How do you see this as affecting your life?

There is an important caveat that comes with this emphasis on teacher-as-discussion-leader in asking students to reflect on their choices, and that is the necessity to remain neutral in tone, in facial expression, in manner, and choice of response. This is not easy, especially when students' ideas and points of view are widely discrepant with what the teacher considers "acceptable" or "appropriate" or even wrong. But if teachers cannot be neutral in these discussions, then what emerges is merely a game that students play to tell the teacher what she or he wants to hear, since students have become expert in "reading" teachers' words, expressions, and postures as indicators of their own viewpoints. Nothing is gained in this kind of charade that enables the promotion of students' examination of their own choices.

There are, of course, exceptions to this caveat and those exceptions lie in the teacher's own values with respect to what he or she considers beyond the pale—areas of great concern in which the teacher feels he or she must take a stand. This is a healthy way of giving evidence that teachers too have values positions that they hold dear; and when a teacher is a true role model for his or her students, that expression of value will carry some weight and give students something more to think about. It is helpful, of course, when such opinions voiced by the teacher are introduced as personal biases and done without reproach to students who believe or think differently.

(A) Some topics that have been suggested as appropriate for these "pencil-and-paper" tasks or open classroom discussions include the following:

- The importance of cell phones
- My favorite class activity
- The importance of a good education
- My favorite out-of-class activity
- My "hero"
- My favorite sport
- The most fun I ever had
- The ugliest thing I've ever seen
- The saddest thing I've ever seen
- The worst thing I ever did was
- The kindest thing I ever did was
- Why we have war
- What is right? What is wrong? How do you know?
- Who tells us what is right? What is wrong?
- Why are there good and bad people?
- What is being happy?
- What was the saddest time for me?
- Who is the meanest person I know?
- What is punishment for?
- What is a crime?
- What is a friend?
- What makes us hate?
- Why do people fight?
- What would I do if I were the teacher?
- Why we tweet?

- What's good about the internet?
- What are some bad things about the internet?
- Why do we believe what we read on the internet or social media?
- Why are some kids bullies?
- What should schools do about bullying?
- How do we learn to care about others?
- What's my favorite computer game?
- What's my favorite after-school activity?
- Who is my best friend? Why do I like him or her?
- What are some important characteristics of friends?
- What do you do when someone insists that he or she is right, when you know he or she is wrong?
- What can you do when you know a friend is in trouble?
- What do you do when a friend takes something of yours and doesn't return it?
- What do you do when you see a friend doing something bad or wrong? Do you tell, or not?
- What do you do when a friend makes a promise to you and then breaks the promise?
- What do you do when your peer group wants to do something that you don't approve of, and they are pressuring you to join in?
- What do you do when you are working in a group and one student wants to dominate the discussion?
- What do you do when all of your friends have a Pokémon Z-Ring Interactive Set and you don't have the money to buy one for yourself?

(B) More sophisticated topics that are more current and more appropriate for examination by older students. Since these topics are more emotionally sensitive, teachers will want to be selective with respect to choosing from this list, or not at all.

- Where I stand with respect to capital punishment
- Where I stand with respect to stem cell research
- Where I stand with respect to immigration
- Where I stand with respect to global warming
- Where I stand with respect to de jure segregation of housing
- Where I stand with respect to the use of torture in obtaining information from prisoners
- Where I stand with respect to federal support for the arts
- Where I stand with respect to welfare for those in need
- Where I stand with respect to gun control

- Where I stand with respect to any restrictions on consuming of junk food
- Where I stand with respect to the use of animals in scientific experiments
- Where I stand with respect to using the internet as a way of connecting to new people
- Where I stand with respect to using the internet as a way of meeting a boyfriend or a girlfriend
- Where I stand with respect to getting the news from a tabloid paper
- Where I stand with respect to supporting a candidate for office who has been accused of a crime?
- Where I stand with respect to the need to protect the environment
- Where I stand with respect to posting shaming photos on a website
- Where I stand with respect to providing aid to those who have lost homes and possessions due to hurricanes
- Where I stand with respect to op-ed articles, editorials, and magazine articles that present various points of view about current issues

(C) For students in secondary school social studies classes

- In designing future immigration laws, how would you decide what groups, if any, should be given preference for immigrating to Canada? How would you decide which groups should be given least preference? How did you determine this?
- The year is 1915. World War I is raging. Your friend Robert is considering enlisting in the army. He asks you to help him decide what to do. What advice would you give him? What data arc you using to make your decision? What values guide your advice to him?
- You are a sixteen-year-old female in the year 1922. You live in the small town of Nelson, British Columbia. You feel repressed by the cultural impositions on women in that society, yet you are concerned about taking any action that would violate the values of your parents. Your friends want you to take a stand and "break free" by going to a dance with them, in a neighboring town. What do you choose to do? What data are you using to base your choice on? What do you see as some likely consequences of your actions? What values do you hold that influence your choice?
- You hold an important governmental position during the years of the Great Depression. What kinds of recommendations do you make to your government to bring relief to the unemployed, hungry, and homeless of your country? What data support your decisions? What values do you hold that influence your choice?

- As a teenager in contemporary society, and faced with a life choice, would you choose a BMW or a university education? How did you make that choice? What values guide that choice?
- You are a student in San Francisco during the outbreak of World War II. The Japanese family who lives next door to you is being taken away to be interned in a camp. What action might you take? What values do you hold that lead you to take that action? What do you see as some potential consequences of what you are proposing?
- What do you suppose was behind the American government's decision to restrict Jewish immigrants from entering the United States during World War II? Where do you stand with respect to those policies? What actions might you have taken if you were a knowledgeable teen at that time? What values guide your action?
- Are works of art worth dying for? In the film *The Train*, many lives are lost to save great works of art from looting by the Nazis. Is this a waste of life? What do you think? What values do you hold that support your choice?
- Who should decide issues of life and death? In the case of an eighty-year-old person who must be put on a life support system to sustain his life, who should make that decision? What do you think? What values support your choice?
- Ronnie contracted AIDS as a result of a blood transfusion. He is being transferred into your school and is scheduled to be enrolled in your science class. Should the other students have the right to know? Should Ronnie have the right to his privacy? What decision would you make? What data have you used to support your decision? What values support your choice? How would your decision be influenced if Ronnie contracted AIDS as a result of his homosexuality?
- Allie has been asked by NBC-TV to be a member of a group of high school students who will discuss "What's Wrong with Central High School?" She believes she has been chosen because she has very strong negative views and because that will make for a more interesting and dynamic show, but not necessarily as a truthful representation of the situation at Central High. What should she do? How would you advise her?
- Based upon your reading of the events that led to the onset of hostilities of World War I, make a list of the decisions made by government leaders of the various countries involved that put the world on an irrevocable war course. As you examine these decisions, think about what values informed those choices. What do these decisions tell you about the quality of thinking behind each? What data support your ideas?

The above suggestions for "pencil-and-paper" tasks or for open classroom discussions can serve as a starting point for students to examine their choices, their value positions, what's important to them, and to do so in the presence of further inquiry, through higher-order questions of their value-oriented choices.

The suggestions below focus on ways in which students can be involved in decision making in classroom and/or school situations that lie outside of the curriculum areas, but are relevant for life in school. These are best done in open class discussions, where students may hear the views of others and where the sharing of different views offers a forum for further exploration.

(D) **Classroom/school management situations requiring student decision making**

- What would be a more suitable way to arrange the desks (or chairs and tables) in this classroom? How would that be an improvement over what we now use?
- What would be some good ways to decide on seating arrangements?
- What would be some good ways in which we might clean up after activity periods?
- What are some suggestions for when the classroom is getting too noisy?
- What are some good ways in which we could keep our library (science, other curriculum area) corner looking neat?
- What actions would you advise the teacher to take if and when students are misbehaving?
- What are some good procedures to follow for going to the bathroom, taking drinks, sharpening pencils, and so forth?
- What are some reasons for having a class pet?
- What are some ways in which we could take care of the pet?
- What are some good plans for reminding students not to litter in the schoolyard?
- What might be a plan for starting a recycling program in the school?
- What are some ideas for a class project to help those in need in our community?
- What are some good ways to help a new student to the class/school become part of our group?
- What are some good ideas for a science project?
- What rules do we need in the classroom? In the school?
- What are some ideas for dealing with students who don't obey the rules?

- What can be done if you see someone in the playground being rude or abusive to another student?
- What are some good ways in which we can help a student in our class who is disabled?
- What are some good rules for using cell phones in school?
- What are some suggestions for helping a student who doesn't have enough money for the field trip?

(E) Other related materials that lend themselves to decision making include whole class discussions centering on children's books, films, TV programs, videos, internet offerings, news articles, magazine articles, and others. Students' responses become more informed in the presence of such questions as: What's the right thing to do? What's good about that? Where do I stand on this issue? What's important to me? What are some potential consequences of this choice? What should be done about this? Such questions give them a chance to reexamine their decisions based on more thoughtful analysis of their choices.

(F) One other source of putting students into positions where they are encouraged to examine issues and make some considered decisions is through the use of "teaching cases." The Case Clearing House in the Faculty of Education at Simon Fraser University has an archive of teacher-written cases that are available online, at no cost, to teachers. See http://www.sfu.ca/education/centres-offices/ec/resources/.html.

It is suggested that the use of cases begin with the students having read the case first, followed by small group discussions on the study questions that are appended to the cases. This is then followed by whole class discussion in which the teacher again uses higher-order questions to promote further thinking and examination of the important issues.

SCENES FROM THE CLASSROOM

Holly Lockwood teaches grade 11 social studies in a secondary school in the East Bay of the San Francisco Bay area. Hers is an elective class, but students each term vie to get a place in it because of her tradition of using the Nuremberg Trials as a role-play experience that culminates the semester's work.

Holly is the one that makes the choices for the roles the students will play and she deliberately chooses students against type—in the expectation that an in-depth study of the role as well as the background stories of the characters will lead to greater awareness of the what and the how and the why of the choices made by the people on trial, and of how the prosecuting and defense attorneys, plus the judges, chose their responses to the disclosures, testimonies and witness statements.

For the roles of the Nazi judges on trial, she chose students who were more sympathetic, empathic, caring, and open-minded. For the witnesses giving testimony about what happened to them during the Nazi regime, she chose more closed-minded, more aggressive, less empathic students. As the students studied their parts, and the background stories of each of the characters, there were more than subtle changes in attitudes, beliefs, and values, more than subtle changes in the decisions that were being made about the people in the trials.

At the conclusion of each semester, as Holly debriefed the students, there was consensus that this experience not only changed their outlooks, but their beliefs and values—more than an opening of awareness, but a stronger commitment to human values. Holly, now in her tenth year of teaching, still receives letters and testimonials from former students who tell her that their experience in the role-playing of the Nuremberg Trials was a turning point in their lives, never to be forgotten.

Chapter 12

Introduction to Designing Projects and Investigations

Project-based learning (PBL) has had a long and singular history in both elementary and secondary education, going back at least to 1942, when Wilford Aikin (1942) published the report of the Eight-Year Study. This long-term field research was initiated by what was then the "Progressive Education Association" with such luminaries as Ralph Tyler, Boyd Bode, Eugene Smith, Erik Erikson, Margaret Mead, and Ruth Benedict, to name a few, as sponsors and contributors. The study involved thirty secondary schools—urban, suburban, and rural—and over 800 students.

The experimental group of about 400 students would be freed from standard course work. The other 400 (control group) participated in normal school activities. The study began in 1932 and continued through 1940. The students in the experimental group, liberated from standard secondary school work as well as college entrance requirements, were free to engage in what researchers called "courses in critical thinking, with an interactive view of learning" so that classes became places of higher-order intellectual experiences.

These students designed projects and investigations that dealt with, for example, "the Maine coast in literature, Philadelphia housing, examples of good and bad thinking ranging from a Supreme Court opinion to a vitriolic editorial, American Negro poetry, plans for a modern house, making a motion picture on conservation, co-operatives, community health, and numerous other subjects of genuine student concern" (Aiken, 42). The students' projects and investigations took many forms—art, musical compositions, original plays, interviews, as well as essays.

The results of this fascinating, yet least appreciated, study found that the students in the experimental group went on to college and "far outstripped the control group in college academic grades and honors" (Featherstone 2007). Where they also far outshone the control group was in their "intellectual traits, reading and cultural habits, leadership and personal and social responsibility" (Featherstone 2007).

It is worth recalling the Eight-Year Study to demonstrate the benefits of the work students are capable of doing in designing projects and investigations.

More than three-quarters of a century later, designing projects and carrying out investigations are more frequently seen in the curriculum area of science, where "science fairs"' invite students to prepare and participate in an exhibit in which their talents as innovators can be displayed and rewarded. Not to disparage that, there are many ways in which students may design projects and carry out investigations in other curriculum areas as well.

These kinds of innovative experiences require that students exercise several kinds of mental operations that include observing, comparing, classifying, making decisions, examining assumptions, gathering, organizing and interpreting data, evaluating results, and, of course, problem solving. In fact, nearly all of the thinking operations identified by Raths (1986) are included in the process of designing projects and carrying out investigations.

It is no wonder, then, that "during the past century, innovation in mechanics, computing technology, medicine and business practices has driven economic growth, raised wages, and helped Americans lead longer and healthier lives" (Greenstone and Looney 2011).

Opening the doors to designing projects and investigations can unleash students' creative and intellectual forces that have, in many teachers' experiences, astonished them. The data, as well as teachers' experiences with project-based learning, suggest that the more students can engage in such activities, the more they are strengthened in their creative and problem-solving abilities and the more skilled they become as potential innovators. This has been more than borne out by the Eight-Year Study.

How does this kind of work enable students to become more intelligent consumers of information? While the means and ends are not obvious, it is the case, however, that when students engage in these higher-order mental functions—all of which must be in play in designing a project or an investigation—the clear result is a sharpening of the intellect, an habituation to the process of data gathering, to selecting in what is relevant, substantive, and true, and selecting out what is irrelevant, unsubstantial, and false. These results too are clearly borne out in the evidence from the Eight-Year Study.

When students undertake to design a project or carry out an investigation, they at first need to be clear about what they wish to do—the clearer the objective, the more what follows will make sense and provide the "road map" for the development of the work. Needless to say, work in this area requires a higher level of cognitive sophistication because there is no one way to solve a problem, design a project, or carry out an investigation. But it has been the experience of many teachers that students, even at primary levels, have shown their ability to succeed, and the results have more than often, delighted their teachers with their intelligence, their competence, their originality, and the depth of their commitment.

Designing projects and investigations can be carried out in nearly every curriculum area—and students should have the option of selecting their own area of investigation, their own project, their own ideas, searching out what is relevant for them, rather than having one assigned by the teacher's mandate.

Experience with designing projects and investigations is much enhanced when students can work together in small, cooperative groups, or even in teams of two, since there is much to be gained from their exchanges of ideas and plans, and much insight to be gathered from each other's feedback. And, of course, working in a group or with a partner is much more satisfying and more fun than working solo. However, a note of caution should be raised: Students do not necessarily learn to work in groups by fiat; successful and productive group work is a learned skill, and this is helped substantially by a teacher's leadership in asking them to reflect on their experience and to make suggestions for improvements for the next group session.

In some instances, students may wish to start with a tentative plan, similar to a road map or story board, before taking action. In other instances, students may embark on the task, without a prior plan, and learn, by doing, that some strategies work and others do not, to be abandoned in favor of new approaches. No one way is recommended, as students with varying skills and aptitudes will find the best ways that serve them to carry out the task. Whichever methods are used, they are often improved through the use of the teacher's higher-order questions in debriefing after the fact.

For example:

- What steps did you take to identify the problem to be investigated? How did you determine its relevance to you?
- How did you approach the task of designing your investigation?
- What was good about that? In retrospect, what could you have changed to improve it?
- What were some difficulties you experienced? How did you deal with them?
- What were some good features of your design? In retrospect, what are some weaknesses?
- How did you decide on a way to demonstrate the completion of your work?
- If you had it to do again, what changes would you make?

When students have acquired the skills to carry out project design and investigations "without a net"—that is, without the step-by-step instruction that is often provided for them—they grow in their autonomy, in their ability to reason, to conceptualize, to be more informed, and, of course, to take the initiative when a problem surfaces. They grow in their respect for themselves as problem solvers, no longer dependent on others to tell them what to do, how to do it, and what to think. In fact, they grow to love their autonomy.

One important facet of designing projects and investigations is the students' decisions about how to demonstrate the completion of their work. Many suggestions for how this may be done is found in the section below. However, above and beyond those ideas, students should be free to imagine and invent their own presentations.

CLASSROOM APPLICATIONS

Younger children may begin work on designing projects and carrying out investigations by:

- Trying to figure out how much air is in a balloon
- Figuring out how the speed of a ball thrown across the room can be measured
- Making a plan for how to measure the heat of an object
- Designing a graph
- Gathering data about the history of the school, the neighborhood, and the city
- Finding the best recipe for making pizza
- Figuring out how goods are transported to the city
- Figuring out where the town (or city's) water comes from
- Figuring out the best method of transportation to a particular geographic site
- Planting an organic garden in the classroom/school yard
- Studying the life cycle of a frog or butterfly
- Determining how many and which articles of children's clothing are made abroad
- Gathering data about the history of one's family
- Comparing prices of essential foods being offered by several markets
- Determining the value of a product being offered on TV
- Designing ways to help homeless people
- Determining how much garbage and waste products are being generated by the school
- Designing ways to respond to the needs of a non-English-speaking family that has moved into the neighborhood
- Designing a computer game or a game for the iPad
- Designing an investigation that shows the history of your school

The following are more sophisticated ideas for projects and investigative activities. It is suggested that before students bring their work to completion, they use a fact-check internet site to ensure that any data being presented in their investigations and projects are accurate and rooted in fact. One such site is ww.factcheck.org, which is a project of the Annenberg Policy Center.

- Design an investigation that would provide information about the differences in immigration laws in 1900 and 2017. When your data have been gathered, organize them so that they tell us more about the different ethnic groups that are settling in the United States today, as opposed to those that came in the beginning of the twentieth century.
- Design an investigation that would give information about how students in grade 12 spent their leisure time.
- Design an investigation that would give information about the kinds of TV commercials that promote consumerism in young children.
- Design an investigation that would give information about how people become homeless.
- Design an investigation that would provide information about how artists earn a living.
- Design an investigation that would provide information on the numbers of First Nations peoples in prison in Canada, in relation to other ethnic groups.
- Design an investigation that would provide information on the numbers of black Americans in prison in the United States in relation to other ethnic groups.
- Design an investigation that would provide information on the illnesses and infirmities of the elderly.
- Design an investigation that would provide information on the ways in which students in your school spend their money.
- Design an investigation that would provide information on new immigrants' experiences in your community.
- Design an investigation that would help young people differentiate truth from falsehood on the internet and social media.
- Design an investigation that would provide information on how students in your school receive information about world events.
- Design an investigation that would provide information about the quality of life of the homeless in your city.
- Design an investigation that would provide information about people with physical disabilities.
- Design an investigation that would give evidence of climate change in your geographical area.
- Design a project that would promote students' awareness of disease prevention.
- Create a better design for promoting recycling in your school.
- Design a project that would provide better news service for the students in your school.

- Design an investigation that demonstrates how students' beliefs influence their decisions.
- Design a project that gives evidence of how physical characteristics influence the way students think about people.
- Design a project that portrays cultural diversity in your community.
- Design a project to demonstrate how tides work.
- Design an investigation to show the growth of a major organization such as Amazon or Facebook.
- Design a project that gives evidence of the treatment of one Japanese-American or Japanese-Canadian family during World War II.
- Design an investigation that examines the role of the House Un-American Activities Committee in 1948–1950 under the chairmanship of Joseph McCarthy.
- Design an investigation to demonstrate the judicial process in your state or province.
- Design an investigation to gather information about children in foster homes.
- Design an investigation to demonstrate the ecological value of bees.
- Design an investigation that gives evidence of how women obtained the right to vote in the United States or Canada.
- Design an investigation that demonstrates how large financial contributions influence the electoral process in the United States.
- Design an investigation that demonstrates the different slants on the news by different media.
- Design an investigation that shows the extent and different uses of cell phones among the students in your school.
- Design an investigation that shows how social media influences student thinking.
- Design an investigation that shows the extent of melting of the polar ice cap over the past hundred years.
- Design an investigation that shows the impact of technology on fishing.

SHOW YOUR STUFF!

The results of such designs and investigations can be displayed in many ways, ways that tap into the many and diverse talents and skills of students. For example:

(a) Audio-visual presentations such as image/sound shows, soundtracks, films, photographs, and YouTube videos characterizing a particular event, issue, or theme of significance

(b) Interviews, personal accounts, oral histories, and recollections

(c) Company study: in-depth analysis of a company tracing its historical development, present situation, and future plans

(d) Writing a case: a form of narrative drawing on information and data from curriculum areas that focus on specific content-related issues

(e) Writing a play or a story

(f) Producing a play or a musical

(g) Producing a podcast

(h) Artwork, sculpting, models, inventions, and cartoons

(i) Books, newspapers, magazines, and journals: literary accounts portraying specific events or period of time

(j) Computer projects: for example, developing artwork, designs, plans, caricatures, newspapers, information packages for self-directed learning, and blogs

(k) Music: the creation of music and lyrics that reflect the values and the political and social climate of a period, or a staged musical production

(l) Designing and carrying out scientific experiments: that is, the creation of credible, reliable, and controlled experiments that involve practice with formulating hypotheses, predicting, data collection, data recording, interpreting and drawing conclusions

(m) Oral presentations: individual and group presentations that reflect students' research, comprehension, and analysis of a particular topic of study

(n) Theater: the reenactment of plays, poetry, reading, and monologues of literary works that reflect social views

(o) Simulations and debates: analysis, interpretation, and presentations of important legal and social issues through role playing or organized debates

(p) Fashion shows and festivals: using clothing, food, music, and visual props to portray trends and changes in social values of specific periods

(q) Field study: active involvement of students in applying the general principles of learning to real-life situations

(r) Community service: participation in service to the community as a way of stimulating learning and social development

(s) Work experience and volunteer work

(t) Field trips: direct investigations by students in the field to gain first-hand experiences

(u) Scrapbooks and manuals: collections of thematic materials to illustrate a particular topic or area of study

(v) Journals and diaries: the composition of diaries and journals that might have been kept by a person living through a particular experience

(w) Biographies and scenarios: personal histories of famous persons outlining their rise to prominence and the accomplishments for which they are well known

(x) Critiques: analyses and evaluation of certain issues, ideas, writings, films, and plays to show an understanding of how these works are viewed by society

(y) Websites: creating a website that promotes a particular idea, or topic, or cause

(Many of the above suggestions come from the work of secondary school teachers Joe Gluska, Steve Fukui, and Richie Chambers, described in their curriculum materials handbook [2000]. They are included with permission from the authors.)

SCENES FROM THE CLASSROOM

Joe G., a grade 11 social studies teacher, was skeptical about using "designing projects and investigations" as a means of evaluating his students' work. A conservative teacher, he had little belief, initially, in students' capabilities and work ethic to do a credible job in such a sophisticated area of competence. So when he decided on this course of action, he did so with some hesitancy.

He began by offering many suggestions for proposed investigations that related to his eleventh-grade curriculum, as well as suggestions for potential ways to demonstrate the completion of their work. He also invited the students to come up with their own ideas. Students could make their own choices about what they wanted to do. As well, the students could work on their own, or in small groups of their own choosing. For Joe, this was a radical departure from his traditional ways of teaching. He had never before considered his students either ready or capable of work on such a high level of independent thinking.

The results were beyond Joe's expectations in every instance. The students produced work in two and three dimensions that were carefully and artfully crafted, and showed considerable intelligence and insight into the issues that were illuminated by the project work. What's more the projects demonstrated a high level of creativity and skill in their productions. Joe could not have been more pleased or more surprised. He had several of the three-dimensional projects in his office, when a fellow teacher came into the room, looked at the students' work with great admiration, and said, "My students would never be able to do this kind of work."

Chapter 13

Introduction to Creating and Inventing

The writers of children's books, Mel and Gilda Berger are frequently invited to classrooms to talk with children about their work and almost without exception, the question arises about how their stories are created: "Where do those ideas come from?" the students often ask. Despite the frequency with which the same question arises, the Bergers cannot respond in a way that makes sense to the children. Ideas come often from "out of the blue"—when they are least expected. Sometimes in the middle of the night. Sometimes when the author is walking on the beach. Sometimes they don't emerge at all, just when the authors had hoped they would arrive in time to meet a deadline.

That is what is so absurdly confounding about creating and inventing; there's no rhyme or reason to how ideas come, where they come from, and what value they have in the long run. But when the creative juices are flowing, there's nothing quite like the experience of it. Sylvia Ashton-Warner, the internationally acclaimed author of *Teacher* (1963, 1986) and many other books, once said, about her creative work, "I just look up from my keyboard and see what's there and I write what I see." Her mind invented scenes, scenarios, and images—and she did not know where they came from either.

Although we cannot expect creations to come to us when bidden, there is no doubt that from our creative juices come new ideas, new stories, new inventions, new remedies, new everything. Sometimes, the "aha" moment comes from a new awareness of something one has seen a hundred times, and is now "seen" for the first time.

Sir Alexander Fleming called his experiences in "discovering" penicillin on the morning of Friday, September 28, 1928, a serendipitous accident. In his laboratory in the basement of St. Mary's Hospital in London, Fleming noticed a petri dish containing Staphylococcus that had been mistakenly left open was contaminated by blue-green mold from an open window, which formed a visible growth. There was a halo of inhibited bacterial growth around the mold. Fleming concluded that the mold had released a substance that repressed the growth and caused lysing of the bacteria.

Marie Curie intuited that the pitch blend she had been working with must contain another highly radioactive element, yet unknown, which she and her husband later called "radium."

There are hundreds of stories of writers, novelists, poets, and playwrights who are unable to tell how their ideas for their creative work spring forth—some mysterious element that occurs, seemingly "out of the blue"—and is worked and worked until a final draft is produced. But the germ of the idea that comes from who knows where is what gives rise to the new, the heretofore unimagined, the radical, the innovations that move our lives forward.

It is a process that cannot be mandated. But like the strawberries of the field, it can be encouraged, and given opportunities to be expressed, without parameters that might inhibit it or prevent its full flowering. As Warner once said to teachers, "You supply the conditions in which creativity can flow."

Is this a form of thinking? Sometimes thinking is described as "imaginative." Imagining takes a readiness and a willingness to leave what is known and mundane behind; it involves inventiveness and originality, a freedom to entertain what is new and different. When we ask students to imagine and invent and create, we cannot ask for supporting data. The imagination goes beyond data, beyond our experiences. To imagine, to invent, and to create are ways of liberating the mind from the routine tasks of the day.

It may be argued that imagining and creating are not true "thinking operations," but it can also be argued that imagining and creating are the means and the practice of taking us to places we've never been; of flying when we thought that was only for birds; of *King Lear*, when we were stuck in the mire of the Middle Ages; of *The Hound of the Baskervilles*, when what we knew before was Wilkie Collins; of *Finnegans Wake*, when what we had before was *Son of the Middle Border*; of *The Rites of Spring*, when what we had before was Pachelbel; and of heart transplants, when what we had before was death.

Perhaps opening the doors to allow students to create and invent is more important today than ever before, since so many of us live in worlds that are bounded by what is *there*—our computers, our cellphones, our tablets—the sharply delineated constraints of our lives. Only teachers can decide whether to give students opportunities to imagine, invent, and create, but if they should choose to do so, they are bound to be happily surprised at what flows from the minds of our youth.

Imagining and creating are at the very heart of language arts. From imagination come stories, poems, plays, and all means of literary inventions. Imagining and creating allow us to push the boundaries of accepted practice into the new and innovative. The greatest gifts of literature come from the brilliant imaginations and the creative efforts of our most cherished writers. But it is not only in that area of the curriculum that creating and inventing may occur. In encouraging students to be more creative and inventive, we may not only hope that new literary masterpieces may one day emanate from their talents but also that new scientific and medical inventions will emerge and that new art will take us by surprise and astonish us with its beauty.

How would students who develop their skills as creators and inventors be more able to differentiate truth from truthiness? The answers are not exact—but it can be argued that when a mind is free to create and invent, it allows us to be more accepting of uncertainty; we are more comfortable living in world where there are no simplistic answers to the most complex questions and issues. We are more ready to suspend judgment.

Carl Rogers (2003) makes the case that the fundamental condition of creativity is that the locus of evaluation is internal. Rogers' theory suggests that the more creative person is not easily influenced by the opinions and ideas of others. These people are more able to make up their own minds. They are leaders in how and what they think and do.

Many examples are offered below—as starting points for teachers to begin thinking about possibilities for their students' levels of experience and the demands of the curriculum—about "supplying the conditions" under which students' creative juices might flow.

CLASSROOM APPLICATIONS

Some suggestions for students at elementary grade levels are the following:

- Imagine being a character in a story. What would that be like?
- Invent a new character for a story that has been read.
- Draw some pictures of a labyrinth, a headache, a panic attack, a bully, a problem, a railroad trip, a view from an airplane, a Halloween mask, baby talk, a bad dream, a good dream, a beautiful garden, a movie poster, a Rube Goldberg invention, a perpetual motion machine, a nightmare, a vibration, summer
- Imagine being a famous rock star. What would your life be like?
- Create a commercial for a favorite snack food.
- Create a poem using only six words.
- Imagine a new way to say:

  - The ugliest thing I ever saw
  - Cool
  - I don't like it
  - I don't understand

- My room is a mess
- I love to go swimming
- I lost my gloves
- I want to buy a man's handkerchief

- Create a short story that is a mystery and would be exciting to read.
- Create a television program that would be suitable for four-year-olds.
- Design a computer game that would make use of puzzles.
- Imagine living on an island where you had no electricity. What would it be like to live there?
- Imagine being a Navajo Indian and living on a reservation.
- Create a poster that would encourage people to take better care of the environment.
- Imagine what it would have been like if you were a sailor on the voyage of Columbus.
- Imagine what it would have been like if you were among the few first immigrants to America who came ashore on Plymouth Rock. Write a poem about it.
- Invent a playground for young children that would be adventurous and safe. Draw some pictures of what it would be like.
- Create some pictures that show how solar energy works.
- Imagine what it would be like to take a trip into space.
- Design your own space ship.
- Create a plan to teach your dog to fetch the newspaper.
- Invent a new toy.
- Invent a rain-making machine.
- Invent a rain-stopping machine.
- Invent a wind-up toy that takes out the garbage.
- Invent a robot that cleans up your room.
- Invent a computer system that takes over most of the chores you dislike.
- Create a habitat for your pet snake. Draw some pictures of it.
- Invent a dog house that has no right angles.
- Invent a way to weigh a giraffe.
- Make up a game with numbers.
- Invent a new way to add fractions.
- Invent a new way to tell time.

For students who are older and more mature:

- Create a plan that would prevent war for all time.
- Imagine what it was like to live on a farm in Oklahoma during the Dust Bowl. Draw a picture or write a poem about it.
- Invent a poster that would inspire teens to embrace more socially responsible values.

- Invent a game for an iPad that would teach magic tricks.
- Invent a font that would be different and attractive for a poster.
- Invent a game to teach simple addition and subtraction to young children.
- Imagine that it is the year 2030 and the requirement of genetic testing of a fetus were made into law. Design a poster that opposes this law.
- Imagine living in 1950 and helping your family building a bomb shelter in your backyard. Write a poem about it.
- Imagine being a Canadian-Japanese citizen and being taken to an internment camp in 1942. Design some illustrations that show life in the camp.
- Imagine being a Native American and being evicted from your land during the westward expansion in the United States. Write a poem or draw some illustrations depicting that eviction.
- Imagine being a partisan in France during World War II. Write a song about your experiences.
- Create a podcast that would help to overcome racism.
- Imagine what it was like when the few people gathered in 1776 to write the Declaration of Independence. Create plans for a debate with two sides, one opposing the declaration and one side supporting it.
- Imagine what it was like to discover DNA. Create a cartoon that depicts that discovery.
- Imagine what it was like when Archimedes discovered water displacement. Create a cartoon that depicts that discovery.
- Imagine what it was like if you were a soldier at Valley Forge during the winter of 1778–1779 during the Revolutionary War. Write a poem, or draw an illustration about that experience.
- Imagine what it was like if you were brought on a slave ship from Africa and were being sold on an auction block to the highest bidder. Write a story about that experience.
- Imagine what Socrates meant when he wrote, "The unexamined life is not worth living." Write a poem about it.
- Imagine what it was like for President Lyndon Johnson to ask the Congress to enact the Civil Rights bill. Draw some cartoons that depict the process.
- Imagine what it was like for President Nixon to resign from his office. Make a collage that depicts that experience.
- Imagine what it was like for Galileo to have to renounce his scientific findings in the face of pressure from the church. Draw some cartoons that depict that experience.
- Imagine what it was like for Ignaz Semmelweis to find that medical doctors refused to accept his theory of antisepsis (germ theory). Write an essay about it.
- Create a storyboard for a TV program that is so compelling that people will stay at home to watch it.

- Create a character for a series of mystery stories that is the rival of Sherlock Holmes. Write the first chapter of a book featuring this character.
- Create a character that would be the equivalent of Harry Potter and would be equally popular. Draw an illustration of the character.
- Imagine being an immigrant aboard a ship arriving in New York City in 1900 and seeing the Statue of Liberty for the first time. Draw an illustration or write a poem about the experience.
- Imagine being an immigrant aboard a ship and arriving in Ellis Island in 1900 and not being able to speak English. Write a story about that experience.
- Imagine being a patient receiving the first heart transplant. Draw some cartoons to demonstrate the process of heart transplants.
- Imagine being a soldier during World War I and given the order to attack from your trench. Draw a picture or write a poem or essay about that experience.
- Imagine what might have happened if, instead of starting World War I, the nations got together and tried to work out their differences. What would the result have been? Write a story about it.
- Imagine what it was like living in India as an Indian under the Raj. Draw a cartoon depicting that time for you.
- Imagine what it was like to be a member of the lower caste (the untouchables) in India. Draw a poster that opposes the caste system.
- Imagine what it would have been like for you to accompany Marco Polo on his travels to the east. Create a map that shows your journey and the hardships that you encountered.
- Imagine what it was like to be dining at the palace of the Pharaoh. Draw an illustration depicting that experience.
- Create a song or a poem that would describe life in your neighborhood.

SCENES FROM THE CLASSROOM

The grade 4 students were asked to create a poster that would inspire teens to develop more socially responsible behaviors. One student wrote,

> *My poster would show three young children, sitting on a carpet in nursery school, asking the rest of us to take care about what we do now, so that the world is a healthy place for them when they grow up. My poster would have captions over each child's head, and the captions would say: (1) Protect our environment by buying what you need and by watching what you throw away. (2) Protect our people by finding better ways than war to solve our problems. (3) Protect ourselves by learning how to live more caringly with each other.*

Chapter 14

Introduction to Evaluating and Assessing

The word *evaluation* contains within it the word *value*—since making evaluations consists of determining the worth of something. What makes evaluation difficult is that those judgments lie in the eyes of the beholder. Thus, when Van Gogh was producing his magnificent works of art, he never, in his lifetime, was able to sell even one of his paintings, except to his brother, who bought them out of kindness and support for him. Yet, a recent sale at Sotheby's brought $20 million for a Van Gogh painting of sunflowers.

Our value judgments of what's good, what's bad, what's important, what's useless, what's sinful, what's immoral, what's selfish, what's noble, what's ethical, and so forth change with the ethos of the times, with the people in power positions who "call the shots," and with the demands of society and the culture. A student's essay, given to five different professors of English, earned five different marks, ranging from C– to A+. Determining value, therefore, is as tenuous as a slippery slope; one treads carefully lest one loses one's footing as standards and mores change with the times, with the culture, and certainly with the eye of the evaluator.

Evaluations are not truths, although many students believe their grades to be accurate representations of what and how they have learned.

Yet, despite the inherent problems in the "squishiness" of evaluative judgments, the need for making those judgments plays an important role in our lives, especially when it comes to matters of choice. In matters of consequence, we normally evaluate before we choose; and in making our choices, we are guided by criteria that inform the evaluations. To complicate matters even further, we remain mindful that our assessments are not fact, but our own hopefully informed awareness of the shaky grounds on which we determine value. The more open we are to those parameters, the more informed our evaluations may be.

Students are often quick off the mark to make judgments about what they like, dislike, hate, scorn, love, and adore, and these are tossed off as easily as yesterday's knickers, without a lot of thought to the kinds of standards that permit such judgments to be of merit. So for teachers to begin to tap into the questions of what upholds students' judgments is a start in the direction of promoting understanding and intelligent thinking about the values that underlie choice. Such skills raise students' awareness in making differentiations between truth and truthiness, between what information is supported by data and what information distorts and manipulates data to win the support of the uninformed.

There is no limit of opportunity to engage students, at every educational level, in making evaluations, determining the value of what is "good" and what is not, including the varying degrees between, from one end of the spectrum to the other. Learning to become aware of the standards that guide those assessments is one important step in becoming more intelligent evaluators.

In this process, it is helpful to remember that questions like "Why do you like that?" or "Why do you think that is good?" are less than productive, for the reason that students may not even know "why." So substituting other more productive questions may be more helpful in bridging the gap between "not knowing" the standards and becoming more aware of them—as students grow in their ability to make more intelligent evaluative judgments. For example:

- You seem to have a high regard for clothes with designer labels. Can you give me some reasons that explain their importance to you?
- You've chosen to read the book *Little Women* three times. There must be some important reasons for you to enjoy that book so much.
- You asked your mother for an iPad for your birthday. Can you tell me what makes this a good gift for you?
- You've told me that you don't listen to the news on TV. You must have some reasons for that decision.
- You've said that people should not give money to beggars who are homeless. You seem to be quite strong in your views about that. Can you tell us about your reasons for that point of view?
- You believe that the postings on social media are an important way of connecting people with each other. I'm wondering if you can tell me about what you see as some downsides of social media.

What's perhaps more difficult than asking the "right questions" is the teacher's role in remaining neutral when students express ideas, values, and opinions that are at an extreme from what the teacher him- or herself believes.

For only when the teacher can maintain that neutral stance will it be possible for students to tell what they really think and what they really believe. That is not to say that teachers should always remain neutral in expressing their views, for there are times when a teacher's values will not only inform but also serve as a role model for students as they develop their own ideas. But it is in the realm of this interactive process that a teacher's role in remaining neutral is key to students' own clarity of how and what they value.

These, of course, are the merest beginnings that enable students to become more informed evaluators. It takes time to develop such skills, and the more students are invited to consider the standards that guide their choices, in the presence of respectful questions and responses of teachers, the more possible it is for them to grow as informed and intelligent evaluators.

One approach that is helpful is to present students with the kinds of foolish and even harmful judgments heard and seen in the social media, in the press, in the supermarket tabloids, and in talk radio, and asking them to make serious and informed evaluations of what they have seen and heard. Using a fact-check site, like www.factcheck.org, is a helpful tool in making those assessments, comparing what is fact and what is disinformation and engaging in discussions that examine how and why some people are so easily fooled into making choices by fiction presented as fact.

In the section that follows, many examples are offered as possible activities in which students can be called upon to make evaluations, and to identify the criteria or standards upon which they are basing their assessments. They are only a small sample of suggestions, and teachers may choose from the group those they believe would correlate with students' levels of competence, and with the curriculum standards of the grade. Ideally, teachers will generate their own ideas, as engaging students in evaluating and assessing can play an important role in daily classroom work.

Evaluating and assessing can be done with "pencil-and-paper" tasks, as well as in open classroom discussion; both venues are appropriate and perhaps one or the other may be particularly applicable to different groups. It may be useful, at first, to begin with some "trial runs," discussions in which students are asked for opinions or points of view about a particular issue.

It may also be helpful to point students to the nature of the operation—that is, to explain to them that they have been involved in the process of evaluating, that this means that they are offering opinions about worth and value, more worthy and less worthy, and good or bad. But what is important underlying such assessments is their ability to specify the criteria, the standards, on which their value judgments are being made. In other words, what are the reasons behind such an opinion?

The operation of evaluating and assessing offers students opportunities to sharpen their critical capabilities, to raise their qualitative standards, to discriminate between the exceptional and the mundane, and to appreciate higher quality. It helps them to move from superficial assessments ("It was good") to a more thoughtful examination of the criteria that allow such judgments to be made.

Because judgments of value lie in the eye of the beholder, it would not be uncommon for one issue, one item, one story, one painting, one poem, and so forth to find fault with some and praise with others. And even sophisticated adults can be seen to have strong differences of opinion about certain items, for example, as seen in readers' comments on a magazine issue:

- I enjoyed it so much.
- It was a brilliant issue.
- Nice experiment, but essentially a failure.
- It took me only thirty minutes to read it.
- I read through it all and it was so satisfying.
- I read it from cover to cover.
- I couldn't put it down.

It was far from unusual that the legendary movie critics Siskal and Ebert differed often in their views about whether to give a film a thumbs-up or thumbs-down.

That is why it is so important for standards to be identified—the standards that guide students' judgments. Otherwise, those judgments are merely knee-jerk responses with little worth. As Adam Kirsch has written, "Democracy relies on a citizenry informed and active enough to make such judgments; in a democracy we are all critics" (2017).

CLASSROOM APPLICATIONS

Language arts is an area rich with possibilities, one that is perhaps a more natural beginning to sharpening students' skills in evaluating. Stories, poems, books, and television programs are familiar territory, and these can be taken from what is available in school and from students' homes. Social studies is another fruitful area for sharpening evaluation and assessment skills. A few suggestions for elementary students are offered below:

- Have the students work in study groups of three to four to make an evaluation of the following poem, by determining what is good about it and what is less than good:

  Don't tell anyone
  but

I have a
fat guardian angel
with an electric halo and
burnt out bulbs. (Nancy Bawden)

- Have the students work together in groups of three to four and ask them to make an evaluation of the following story that was written by a student in another class. Ask them to work together and think of what might be said to the writer of the story to help him or her improve.

The Yo-Yo Family. My family is red. They live in the sewer. The eat slugs and worms. They can't talk because they are deaf.

- Ask the students to work together in a small group to discuss how they are able to decide if a movie or a TV program is good or bad. What do they look for in deciding the qualities of "good" or "bad"? What criteria are being used?
- Ask the students to work together in a small group to discuss what criteria they use before they decide on what computer game to buy.
- Ask students to work together in a small group to discuss:

  - What are students' favorite subjects in school? What criteria are they using in making that determination?
  - What are students' favorite foods? What criteria are being used in making that evaluation?
  - Who is a student's "idol"? What is it about that person that makes him or her of merit to the student?
  - How do students make a selection about the kinds of shoes they want to buy? What criteria are they using in making that assessment?
  - What is a student's favorite Saturday morning activity? What is it about that activity that makes it a favorite?
  - What's important about having rules in class? What are some ideas about that?
  - What do students consider to be the nonpareil standards for a good friend? What does a friend have to do in order for him or her to be crossed off one's list of a "good friend"?
  - What makes your neighborhood a good place to live? What do you consider to be a "good place to live"?
  - What kinds of running shoes are the best ones to buy? What makes you think that's true?
  - What's important about being a good sport? What make you think that is true?
  - What would be a good choice for a class field trip? What makes you think that is true?

- What's so important about taking care of our environment? What makes you think that is true?
- Which animals make the best pets? What makes you think that is true?
- Why should students have to learn their multiplication tables? What makes you think that is true?
- What is the most important issue that we are facing today? What makes you think that is true?
- Which source of news gives the most accurate reports of events? What makes you think that is true?

Middle and secondary students may be offered more sophisticated tasks in making evaluations and assessments. However, it should be an *a priori* condition of these activities that students make assessments on the basis of gathered information so that their evaluations are based on data, rather than as facile judgments.

- Determining criteria for evaluating a TV news broadcast or a podcast.
- Generating criteria for assessing quality medical care for elderly patients.
- Generating criteria to evaluate the immigration policy in Canada or the United States.
- Generating criteria that would help in the identification of "what is good art."
- Generating criteria for what is considered equal treatment under the law for people of all races, religions, and ethnic groups.
- Generating criteria for the assessment of the government's treatment of the poverty stricken during the Great Depression under the Hoover administration.
- Generating criteria to identify "moral and ethical" values.
- Determining criteria for evaluating an editorial or an op-ed essay from a local newspaper.
- Determining criteria for establishing an immigration policy for the twenty-first century.
- Determining criteria for evaluating Great Britain's opting out of the European Union.
- Determining criteria for evaluating the success of the United Nations with respect to its charter.
- Determining criteria for writing a successful short story, novel, or play.
- Determining criteria for addressing the local government's position on homelessness in your city.
- Determining criteria for evaluating the presidency of Abraham Lincoln.
- Determining criteria for evaluating the importance of the Magna Carta.
- Determining criteria for evaluating the importance of the Bill of Rights.
- Determining criteria for evaluating the success of the Harry Potter series of books.

- Determining criteria for evaluating the food at McDonald's.
- Determining criteria for who should get the next Nobel Peace Prize.
- Determining criteria for assessing the US government's treatment of Native Americans during the westward expansion in the nineteenth century.
- Determining criteria for assessing the success of the Crusades.
- Determining criteria for assessing the policy for the immigration of Chinese into Canada and the United States in the late nineteenth and early twentieth centuries.
- Determining criteria for assessing the repression of thinking during the Middle Ages.
- Determining criteria for assessing the importance of the invention of the printing press.
- Determining criteria for assessing the importance of our information technology world.
- Determining criteria for assessing the successes and failures of the Third Reich.
- Determining criteria for keeping animals in captivity.
- Determining criteria for assessing the successes and failures of the Russian Revolution.
- Identifying criteria that assess the "electric shock treatment" of mute soldiers suffering from battle fatigue during World War I.
- Identifying criteria to assess the value of the work of Alan Turing in his invention of the first computer as a means of decoding Nazi messages during World War II.
- Identifying criteria to assess the execution of soldiers during World War I who were found guilty of desertion.
- Identifying criteria to assess the treatment of "Okies" who set off for California to escape the Dust Bowl and who were refused admittance to the state.

Some final words must be said about the operation of evaluating and assessing before moving on because we are all critics and we engage in this act often without a lot of thought and without critical regard to what it means, and how it affects not only us but also those to whom the criticism is addressed. So perhaps some words of caution should be raised—that if and when we do learn to use evaluation and assessment with a mind to criteria that are rooted in accurate data, we do that with humanity and with some appreciation for the person or persons at the receiving end of the exercise.

SCENES FROM THE CLASSROOM

She is sitting at the table across from him and he watches her marking the fifth-grade spelling tests. Her eyes scan the twenty words in the left-hand column, guided by her pen, which trails down the row, leaving large red Xs across each of the misspelled words. Without missing a beat, she shifts to the right-hand column and marks red Xs on more words. Then she counts up the Xs in both columns. Twelve. With a sigh, she writes a large 12/40 in the top right-hand corner of the paper, while glancing at the pupil's name on the next paper to undergo a similar vigorous assault. Trying not to be intrusive, he continues to watch her marking paper after paper, slashing through the incorrect words like karate chops. Bim, bam, bang! Counting up. Sighing. Recording the incorrect numbers at the top of the page and headlining in bold numbers, the extent to which each child has erred.

The next paper yields a tally of eighteen incorrectly spelled words out of forty. The paper is a bloodbath of red slashes. He can't help wondering if the mark is more than just an indication of how many words are correct and how many are wrong. Is it possible that this kind of evaluation has a punitive dimension?

Perhaps some of the teacher's obvious distress over the students' poor performance comes from her own feelings of disappointment that "the children have let her down." She has, after all, taught the lesson. Perhaps she believes the students have betrayed her by not learning well what she worked so hard to give them? Might the angry red marks represent the way she would like to punish the students for disappointing her? Is it possible that some evaluative judgments are clouded by unrecognized feelings about persons, situations, issues? Is it possible that evaluations are sometimes used to punish, to disparage, to penalize, to condemn, rather than as a means of identifying weaknesses and strengths, based on clear and reliable standards?

(Adapted from Selma Wasserman (1989) "Learning to Value Error," *Childhood Education* 65, no. 4.)

Section III

Chapter 15

Dealing with Students' Deeply Held Beliefs

There are many ways that we, from our early years, learn to protect ourselves and to fulfill our basic needs. Young children, who are lucky to have warm and loving parents, know to seek solace, comfort, and protection in the arms of their caregivers. Even adults know to whom to turn when the need for comfort and reassurance looms large. These are some of the basic ways in which humans have learned to deal with the adversities of life.

But not every person has someone to whom to turn for help. And not every person has emerged from early childhood experiences as emotionally healthy and "whole." Given the troubled roots of some children, they create, in order to cope, defense mechanisms that become part and parcel of their emotional makeup, intended to protect and comfort them in times of need. These defense mechanisms can be innocuous, or they can be extreme—in either case, the bottom line is that they are far from fail-safe devices; they neither protect nor do they comfort—but once in place, they are hard to relinquish.

In the film *As Good as It Gets* (1997), Jack Nicholson plays the role of an accomplished and best-selling author, with an obsessive-compulsive character disorder that he is unable to shed. There is no obvious threat to his life, yet he must bring his own plastic utensils to the restaurant in lieu of the restaurant's tableware and arrange them in the correct position on his table; he must fold his napkin in just the right way and place it in the right space; he may not step on the cracks on the sidewalk when he walks down the street.

None of this makes sense to anyone with him, but to him, they seem to represent a matter of life and death. So deep is his anxiety and his use of these devices to protect himself that they border on the pathological. These defense mechanisms are not under his conscious control; and they are more extreme when he feels under threat or in stress.

111

Even those of us who do not fall into the category of "obsessive-compulsive" use defense mechanisms for many reasons, often unconscious means of avoiding disaster or keeping us safe. We may "knock on wood" to avoid trouble; we may want to double-check locks, appliances, and switches before leaving the house; we may spend more time than necessary washing up or arranging things in a particular order; and we may have an extraordinary fear of germs that makes us want to keep washing our hands.

Some people believe that something bad will happen if they throw anything away—and become excessive hoarders. Some become compulsive buyers. The list of defensive behaviors that we use to "protect" ourselves from harm and keep us safe is many and varied, but whatever reactive behaviors have been put in place, they neither protect us, nor do they keep us safe. However, there is a huge disconnect between the behavior and the reality.

Related to but not in the same category as obsessive-compulsive behavior is the way some children and adults as well develop strong and pervasive beliefs that serve as defense mechanisms that are hardwired into their emotional makeups. These beliefs have little or nothing to do with rational thinking; but like the beliefs that avoiding stepping on the cracks in the sidewalk will protect one from harm, such pervasive beliefs seem, irrationally, to keep us from coming unglued. There is no rational reason for believing them; but we, nevertheless, maintain a grip on them that is surreal. And they influence our lives in ways that are often counterproductive as well as unreasonable.

Kahneman (2011) suggests these kinds of beliefs are products of System 1 thinking, in which the bias to believe makes people vulnerable to empty persuasive messages such as commercials, slogans, and admonitions from emotive orators. He also suggests that without putting into operation the intelligent habits of mind that come from System 2 thinking, "people will believe almost anything" (81).

Not only that, but the more closed a person's belief system is, the more resistance that person will put up to shedding old convictions and replacing them with new belief systems. As odd as it sounds, such closed belief systems are also mechanisms used to avert danger, to protect us from harm, and to keep us from feeling alone, isolated, and helpless in a world that appears threatening to selves.

According to Rokeach (1960), "As the need to ward off threat becomes stronger, the cognitive need to know becomes weaker, resulting in more closed belief systems" (68). That is why some people favor uncritical acceptance of suggestions and exaggerations of the likelihood of extreme and improbable events. And that is why people who cling to such beliefs as mechanisms to protect themselves are impervious to facts. There is the tendency to cherry-pick facts that confirm deeply held beliefs and reject those that are in conflict with them—using "confirmation bias" to deliberately search for confirming evidence.

Not only does this mind-set prevent children and adults from examining, considering, and incorporating data that contradict those deeply held beliefs, they also are in the unhappy position of being highly defended and closed about their own personal positions, unable to view themselves from a critical and reality-based perspective. Self-awareness is not their strong suit.

Rokeach (1970) describes these primitive belief systems as "extremely resistant to change" (180). They arise from deep personal experience; they are incontrovertible and they are believed regardless of whether anyone else believes them. The example comes to mind of the man who is in therapy because of an acutely diminished sense of self-worth. He is questioned by his therapist, who confronts him with the fact that he has just won the Nobel Prize. To which the man responds by saying, "See, I've fooled them too."

Other beliefs may arise from our identification with certain authorities, reference persons, or reference groups. From them, we "decide" whom we can trust and whom we believe we cannot trust. Inconsequential beliefs are generally easier to change than other kinds of beliefs—but we generally resist changing all our beliefs because we get comfort in clinging to the familiar and because all our beliefs seem to serve highly important functions for us (Rokeach, 183).

It's possible to cite dozens of examples of how deeply entrenched beliefs lead to behaviors in some that others might consider bizarre. While it is true that people with abnormal personality disorders may have their share of bizarre beliefs, such odd beliefs are not limited to psychological dysfunctionality. For example, in a small New England town, 1,500 people gathered to talk about their having been abducted by aliens.

According to an ABC poll, about forty million Americans say they have seen, or have met, someone who has seen an unidentified flying object (UFO) (Chang and Dubreuil 2009). There are people who turn to the Horoscope pages in the newspapers to make decisions about their lives based on "what the stars tell them." Beliefs in ghosts, spirits, and other psychic experiences drive people to fortune tellers, readers of Tarot cards, and clairvoyants.

But beyond those extremes, we may hold beliefs that are more mundane, but nevertheless do not hold up under critical examination. We may hold beliefs about people of color, about certain religious groups, about political parties, about leaders, about celebrities, about clothes, about appearance, about newspapers, about TV news commentators, what is found on social media, about vaccinations causing autism, and about authority figures.

Very young children may have some primitive beliefs about ghosts and goblins hiding under their bed and images that emerge from behind the TV screen, but these more primitive beliefs wane as children grow to maturity.

However, immature and primitive beliefs do not explain the underlying factors that bring people to believe what they believe and cling to those beliefs
in the presence of data that are contrary. In other words, "don't confuse me
with the data; I know what I believe."

Teachers with students who hold deeply entrenched "outré" beliefs will
have their work cut out for them, in trying to "open" such closed-mindedness.
For as has been demonstrated, confronting closed-mindedness with "facts" is
not the best route to open minds. There is the tendency to select only those
data that confirm beliefs (confirmation bias) and to find ways of disregarding
data that are discrepant with the deeply held beliefs. So other strategies need
to be employed—and the bad news is that none of them is a guarantee of success. Nor are they amenable to the "quick fix."

Having confessed to all of that, there is still hope for teachers who want to
try to address these conundrums.

CLASSROOM APPLICATIONS

At first, it is important to admit that dealing with students' belief systems
that are hardwired, and deeply embraced, is one of the big challenges that
teachers can face. There is a huge temptation to face up to the challenge,
confront the student, and let him or her know that such beliefs are not only
unfounded, but also unreal, and, perhaps more to the point, ignorant. That's
about as helpful as putting cups on a corpse—as one's grandmother liked to
remind her grandchildren.

But moreover, such an approach may also damage any shred of a relationship the teacher has with that student, for how is he or she to trust someone who
has mocked, confronted harshly, and even ridiculed him or her? So the first step
in the long process of enabling a student to open a closed mind is the building
of trust in the teacher-student relationship. Without that, there is little or no
hope of that student letting down the defenses that keep those beliefs in place.

Keeping in mind that behind such irrational beliefs is the unrecognized
and unconscious notion that such a system is necessary for the person's well-
being, it follows that any rebuttal or dismissal of those beliefs may be seen as
a threat to that person's self, and to the functional dynamic of his or her life.
It may also be the case that in holding onto unpopular beliefs there may be
elements of guilt or shame. With that awareness as the framework for what
can be done, some suggestions are offered for enabling students to reexamine
their positions, in a safe and supportive environment, that allows them to
move slowly to open minds heretofore closed.

(a) The *theory of cognitive dissonance* was formulated by Leon Festinger
    in what in educational circles is considered the dark ages (1958). Since

then, however, the term "cognitive dissonance" has evolved to become a strategy that is commonly used to confront people with contradictory data that rebut their beliefs, by putting them into situations that become, for them, difficult to sustain, and often, cognitively uncomfortable.

Festinger describes "cognitive dissonance" as a motivating state for humans. He goes on to define "dissonance" as "harsh, jarring, grating, unmelodious, inharmonious, inconsistent, contradictory, discrepant" (512)—in other words, putting two things together that are disharmonious or unpleasant. The two things, when put together, do not fit—"two cognitions are dissonant with each other." Festinger's theory goes on to state that when a person is in a state of cognitive dissonance, he or she must move to reduce or eliminate that dissonance. That is the "motivating factor," the need to remove oneself from the dissonant state.

Arguably one of the most discrepant events in history was the uplifting spirit of the British troops and the great patriotic fervor that walked with them as they marched to the trenches in 1914 at the beginning of World War I. There was joy in the streets and smiles on the faces of the soldiers and their families who cheered them on. After four years of the most obscene, needless slaughter in the history of warfare, after four years of life in the trenches, that patriotic fervor was replaced with a sense of hopelessness, futility, and despair. No soldier who lived through the trench warfare of World War I maintained any illusion of patriotism. Those beliefs were shattered with the relentless bombardment of the cannon and the folly of leaving the trench to gain a few yards. However, it doesn't take a war to confront people with the dissonance that requires them to reexamine their beliefs and replace them with other scenarios.

Festinger (1958) wrote about a group of people who had predicted that, on a given date, a catastrophic flood would overwhelm most of the world. "This prediction of the flood had been given to the people in direct communication from the gods and was an integral part of their religious beliefs" (516). The people in the group believed that those who were *chosen* were to be picked up by flying saucers before the flood occurred. Some of these believers were college students. Some of the people gathered together in the home of one of them. Some of them went individually to their own homes.

On the date that the flying saucer was supposed to land in the backyard of one of the members of the group, they waited, but no flying saucer came. Despite continuing waiting, through the cold night until early morning, no flying saucer arrived. The group struggled to understand what happened, trying to find some explanation that would enable them to hold onto their beliefs, in the presence of contrary, dissonant data.

Those members of the group who stayed together as a group found ways to "explain" the absence of the rescuers in a "message" that came from God, stating that he had saved the world and stayed the flood. Those members of the group who had gone, individually to their own homes, without the support of the other members of the group, became nonbelievers (Festinger 1958, 515–16). The two groups found different ways to overcome the dissonance.

The group members who continued to hold their original belief in the flood and in the rescue by the flying saucers brought the dissonance to a close by the assumption of the "message from God who had saved the world from the flood." The members of the group who did not have the support of the group to sustain their original belief abandoned the belief altogether. The study sheds light on how group support, or peer influence, plays a role in sustaining a belief and how, without that, an individual must confront a discrepant belief on his or her own.

What does all of this tell the teacher who might consider using "cognitive dissonance" as a method of confronting students with beliefs that are illogical, ill-informed, pernicious, hurtful, and, sometimes, downright malicious?

If "experience is the best teacher," one obvious way is to inject a cognitively dissimilar experience into their lives, one that would place them in a situation not unlike the one in which the group who believed in the flood to end the world. And the more real the experience is, the more impact it is likely to have. Second-stage experiences, like watching a film or a TV show, or reading a story, or examining historical events, are useful as well, but do not carry the same power. Consider, too, the use of peer groups as another means of providing support for and giving credence to the discrepant experience.

There may be levels of defensiveness in students who hold beliefs that are pernicious—and that defensiveness is part and parcel of the closed-mindedness that allows them to sustain those beliefs. And to approach such defensiveness with open confrontations is not only not healthy, but also counterproductive. When a teacher has a true rapport with students, when students know they can trust him or her, that carries a lot of weight in helping to shift students' beliefs. When the teacher is truly genuine in his or her interactions with students, that too is a powerful operating force in asking students to reexamine their beliefs in the presence of contrary experiences.

None of this is easy, and these strategies are, alas, not guarantees. But the alternative is not to try, not to attempt to break through the chains that bind students' ideas and keep their minds closed to what is real.

In an affirmation of the way this might work in practice, one teacher recalled his secondary school social studies class, in which the eleventh graders were studying the internment of Japanese-Canadian citizens during the outset of World War II. In one small study group he was observing, one boy took the position, and made a strong effort to defend his view, that "the Japanese got what they deserved, since, after all, they bombed Pearl Harbor."

The other six members of the group argued against his claim, but to no avail. He was convinced that he was right and found ways to ignore or subvert the arguments of his group.

It was only after the groups had reconvened to whole class discussion that this student, and several others, raised their belief—that it was "right" that Japanese-Canadian citizens were taken from their homes, their belongings left behind, and carted off to internment camps far afield from their places of residence, when a Japanese-Canadian fellow student spoke softly to say, "I have the dreadful feeling that if this were happening to me and my family today, none of you would stand up for us," that the discrepancy between the original belief and the reality of the situation was brought home.

Students who before could not be persuaded by data were now confronted by the human face of the situation—someone they knew and cared about—and that was the turning point that opened closed minds.

(b) *Using higher-order questions* in a group discussion is one method that has been advocated by many in the teaching profession to address the nature of student thinking (Bloom 1956; Christensen 1987; Wassermann 2009, 2017). In some sources, these were called "clarifying questions"—those teacher responses that bring an element of cognitive dissonance into a classroom discussion (Raths, Harmin, and Simon 1973; Simon 1973). Used selectively, such "clarifying" or higher-order questions can introduce a note of dissonance into a student's naïve, illogical, or wrong-headed belief, and bring about a reexamination of that belief. Used inappropriately, it can backfire, raise levels of defensiveness, and tightly secure the closed-mindedness.

The differences between what works and what fails to work is a combination of the teacher's genuineness, his or her level of trust with students, the nature of the teacher-student relationship, and the interpersonal dynamic during the questioning. A student who trusts a teacher, who perceives that teacher as genuinely supportive and caring, who has had a strong relationship with that teacher, and who does not feel under attack during the interpersonal interactions is more likely to benefit from the teacher's use of higher-order questions that require that student to reexamine securely held belief systems.

The bottom line, in such an interactive dialogue, is that the student may not feel threatened, under attack, or shamed by what he or she believes, and that the interaction be played out so that the student feels safe in that cognitive examination. Moving a student's thinking from tightly closed to more open takes more than a scalpel, or a hatchet; it takes skill, finesse, and patience. And more often than not, more than one set of dialogues.

Some examples of clarifying or higher-order questions that can be used to bring students to that point of reexamination are the following:

- You seem to have thought about that a lot. Can you tell me where those ideas came from?
- This seems to me to be something you care about a lot. Am I interpreting that correctly?
- Perhaps there are some actions that you've taken with regard to that belief. Can you tell me more about that?
- I wonder if you've considered any alternatives.
- This seems to me something that is very important to you. Have I understood that correctly?
- I wonder how you know that that (idea) is right.
- Is this a belief that you've decided for yourself? Or from someone else?
- Is this a new idea for you? Or have you thought about this for a long time?
- I wonder what you see as some consequences of that belief. Can you explain it to me?

Questions and responses such as these ask the student to put his or her ideas under scrutiny. It is unlikely that those beliefs or ideas will change in that instant; rather, they give the student something to think about, something to consider, and something to wrestle with as he or she attempts to resolve the dissonance that they create. So nothing like an "ah-ha" moment is likely to occur, rather a route to further consideration, further thinking, further examination, and perhaps more clarifying or higher-order questions and responses along that pathway.

(c) *Role-playing and "problem stories"* have been used by many teachers, at all educational levels to address critical issues in the curriculum and give students opportunities to consider and reconsider their own beliefs in structured situations. (See, e.g., chapter 11, describing one teacher's use of the Nuremberg Trials to confront students' beliefs.)

Role-playing is one medium that gives students an opportunity to act as characters in situations that highlight selected dilemmas. These dilemmas may come from historical events, such as the Nuremberg Trials, or from situations that are relevant to students' in-class or out-of-class experiences, organized by the teacher. For example:

George is a new boy in school and in the neighborhood. He comes from Malta and doesn't know much English. He's shy and is worried that his new classmates won't like him.

As Shaftel and Shaftel (1967, 1982) describe it, "Role playing is a transactional process; it stimulates both the emotive and analytic aspects of thinking as students learn to express ideas spontaneously, to listen to the ideas of others, and to develop respect for themselves and others" (11).

Shaftel and Shaftel's seminal text was written in 1967 and republished in 1982. Even today, many years later, it is still considered a classic in what it professes and in the many examples that can be adapted for classroom use. In such structured situations, students have an opportunity to examine their own beliefs through the lens of a selected significant event, in which personal experiences are highlighted and explored. "The teacher, in these situations, works to develop a climate in which it is safe for students to try out all ideas, even those that are not expedient and not socially acceptable or are even anti-social. Each is a reality to be actually tested in a public arena (the enactment)."

The focus on these enactments is not on arriving at right answers but on open inquiry. Both teacher and group listen to each other with full attention. The teacher models this behavior by probing with such questions as "if I understand you, you are saying that." And a child can say, "Yes, that's what I mean," or "No, I mean." The observing class is asked to listen and watch carefully so as to be able to respond to a proposal in terms of how are people feeling? Who is affected? Could this really happen? What will happen now? (14).

The Shaftels further add that "the teacher who is unafraid to say, 'You two seem to have opposing ideas of what happened (or what will work), can we explore these differences and try to understand how each of you has come to your opinions?' is guiding students to respect individuality" (14).

As students learn to consider consequences, by taking a position in a role and playing out how it feels to be on the receiving end of an action, such pseudo-life experiences can and do have lasting effects on beliefs, thinking, and behavior. Thus, students have a chance to learn to become more empathic with each other, more caring, more considerate, and more thoughtful, as well as having rich experiences in examining their beliefs, and reflecting on what they value and what decisions guide their actions.

Role-playing carried out wisely, thoughtfully, and with careful consideration presents students with deeply affecting structured situations that can have profound effect on who they are and on what they believe.

MORE SUGGESTIONS FOR CLASSROOM APPLICATION

The Shaftels outline a process for carrying out role-playing that is offered below and that may be helpful for teachers who wish to initiate these kinds of experiences for students to examine their belief positions:

* *Initiate a study: as a means for immediate involvement.*
* *Delineate a problem: which then demands a follow-up of data collecting, reorganization of information, and testing of ideas. In this way, students can be inducted into in-depth studies.*

- *Develop empathy: help students in any study to involve themselves in the affective as well as the cognitive aspects of an area through exploration of specific people in delineated situations. For example, how would it feel to indenture yourself for seven years to an unknown master in order to get passage on a boat to the New World?*
- *Stimulate communication: between students and between students and teachers. It is easier to express ideas in the safe environment of role-playing than to risk yourself in the arena of abstract ideas. Opinions flow freely from discussions of enactments during the role-playing sequence.*
- *Create an awareness of the need for skills: as students are confronted with situations (how to interview an expert, for example), the need for specific skills training becomes immediately apparent.*
- *Teach elements of problem solving: when first confronted with a problem situation, students tend to reach for simplistic solutions. As the teacher encourages alternative proposals for resolving a difficulty, the complexity of situations is revealed, the need for alternative thinking emerges, consequential analysis is encouraged, and students can be inducted into problem solving in action.*
- *Stimulate moral development: as students face moral and ethical dilemmas, the problem-solving process of role-playing, with focus on who is involved, how the decisions proposed affect each person, and how each one feels, helps the participants achieve growth in moral development.*
- *Stimulate the decision-making process: as personal-social dilemmas are presented, or community action situations delineated, students engage in decision making at a level that is meaningful to them (Shaftel and Shaftel 1982, 10–11).*

The Shaftels offer dozens of examples of role-playing taken from the real-life experiences of students, which cut across several curriculum areas, and which are also appropriate for students at all levels of school (Shaftel and Shaftel 1982, 153–341). The reenactment of historical events offers a rich repertoire of possibilities for intermediate- and upper-grade students.

Before embarking on such a course of action, it is recommended that students prepare themselves with background data so that when they do reenact the event, they do so from knowledge, rather than from fantasy. It is a given that students will be required to defend a particular point of view from a position that is rooted in data, thereby strengthening their beliefs. That is why the strategy of assigning students roles that run counter to their own beliefs can serve as a wedge for the reexamination of those beliefs. It is also a given that through such dialogues and debates, steeped in a background of historical data, students will gain deeper perspectives of historical events. A few examples of critical issues in history are offered below:

- Athenians in power positions (399 BC) see Socrates and his methods of using reason to challenge traditional ideas as corrupting youth. Looking for a scapegoat, the authorities accuse him of failing to honor the gods and condemn him to death. You are on the jury to decide about the fate of Socrates.
- Opposition to Caesar in the Roman Senate grew stronger, despite his many contributions to the advancement of the Roman Republic. Senators denounced him as a tyrant who was destroying the Republic. Others applauded his reforms that strengthened Rome. You are in the Roman Senate and are arguing for and against the rule of Caesar.
- In 1095, at the Council of Clermont in southern France, Pope Urban preached a crusade against enemies of the church. Christian knights, he urged, must rescue the holy land from the Muslims. "If you undertake this journey," he claimed, "and if you die on the crusade, your sins will be forgiven." Thus, thousands of peasants and knights sewed crosses to their clothes, and set out to loot towns in eastern Europe and attack and kill non-Christians, slaughtering Muslim and Jewish men, women, and children. You are in a group of peasants who are arguing for and against joining the crusades.
- You are in a small group arguing for and against child labor in England in the nineteenth century. The owners of factories argue that child labor is essential to produce material that is required for the national interest and for the economy. Others argue that child labor is inhumane and wish to initiate laws against it.
- Ludwig Semmelweiss is convinced that childbed fever is caused by infection and that doctors should wash their hands before undertaking surgery. He is mocked by the learned doctors in the medical association for his unfounded views. You and others make the arguments to oppose and support Dr. Semmelweiss.
- A group of delegates from nine colonies met in New York to protest the Stamp Act that taxed a variety of items from newspapers, deeds, and wills, to dice and playing cards. You are in a group of people that is arguing for and against declaring the thirteen colonies of America independent of British Rule.
- You are in a group of advisors for President Lincoln arguing for and against a war against the southern states and the signing of the Emancipation Proclamation.
- On June 28, 1914, Archduke Francis Ferdinand, heir to the throne of Austria-Hungary, is assassinated in Sarajevo. Tensions build between the

European states, and escalate to the verge of war. Diplomats race across Europe desperately trying to find a peaceful solution to the crisis. You are in a group of diplomats representing several sides, advocating for and against a war to settle the differences.

- In 1937, Mr. Churchill sees Adolf Hitler as a proponent of war and is advocating in the British Parliament that the United Kingdom prepare itself for such an eventuality by building up the military. Opponents to Mr. Churchill and those who despair of the possibility of another war are desperately trying to calm the waters and remain detached from what is happening in Europe, as Hitler marches across the continent, invading and annexing territories and claiming them as part of Germany. You are in a parliamentarian debate arguing both sides of the issues.
- Some other critical events/issues that lend themselves to role-playing are the following:
- The Cuban Missile Crisis and President Kennedy's advisors in debate.
- President Herbert Hoover's advice for and against the attack on the Bonus Army Marchers in Washington, DC, in 1932.
- President Truman's advisors for and against the use of the atomic bomb to end the war in Japan in 1946.
- Bridget Bishop is on trial in Salem, Massachusetts, in 1692, accused of being a witch. If convicted, she will be hanged. You are on the jury to deliberate her guilt or innocence.
- Susan B. Anthony, a suffragist, took it upon herself to vote in 1872, despite the fact that women had not been granted voting rights. The Supreme Court is debating whether to find her guilty. The members of the court are debating her case.
- During World War II, with thousands of American men in the armed forces, women were called on to fill much needed jobs in war industry. Heretofore thought as being the "weaker sex," women now took positions on the assembly lines, doing work that was always considered "a man's job." When the war was over, and men returned from fighting, women were now expected to return to their homes and take their place once again in the kitchen. You are on a panel deliberating whether women should be allowed to remain in their wartime jobs in peacetime, or whether they should be fired so that the returning veterans could replace them.
- It is 1964 and your school is organizing groups of students to join the Civil Rights march in Washington, DC. On the one hand, joining the march might be dangerous; on the other hand, the issue is important to you. Your class is debating whether to join the march.

The suggestions for classroom activities are not iron-clad guarantees that if and when used, students will promptly and with ease, shift their strongly held but inappropriate beliefs toward those more rooted in fact. With some students, reexamination of belief positions may evolve over time—sometimes weeks, sometimes months. With some students, and this is rare, there may be an "ah-ha" moment, when the "light" goes on and the student sees more clearly where his or her belief has been wanting.

With other students, shift in beliefs may not be seen at all. In fact, there are cases in which strongly held, but dysfunctional, beliefs are even more deeply engrained and endure through adulthood.

So should any of these strategies be attempted, given that the chances of success are not 100 percent guaranteed? Does the doctor proceed with the operation when the chances are not guaranteed of total success, but when there is only a good chance?

As in any other situation, the teacher is the key—the person to decide. But when and if the strategies do work to help students to open their minds, discarding and abandoning beliefs that have been counterproductive in their lives, the joy of seeing that change may be more than worth the effort.

SCENES FROM THE CLASSROOM

The principal came into her room to observe her lesson. She, a first-year teacher, had her ideas about teaching and learning shaped by her reading about "teaching for thinking" and her more progressive professional development experiences at her university. For this first supervisory visit, she was going to demonstrate how her grade 3 students were able to work effectively in groups, carrying out scientific investigations with the concepts of "sinking and floating" objects.

Each group of four children was working at a table with a large plastic pan of water, and a variety of objects, which they were testing to find which were "sinkers" and which were "floaters" and whether they could turn sinkers into to floaters. The children were busily engaged with their experiments, and she walked around the room, watching, and raising a few questions that triggered further thinking about their investigations.

The principal sat in the back of the room, looking at his watch, as if he were expecting something more to happen. After about fifteen minutes, he got up, turned to her, and said, "I'll come back when you're teaching."

Chapter 16

Using Questions and Responses That Promote Further Examination of Issues

The Interactive Dialogue

"I think that all candidates for political office lie so I would vote for the one who is the most obvious liar," the man stated his position without any sense of irony.

What's the best response to this statement?

Teachers who engage students in expressing their beliefs, in giving responses to thinking activities, and in presenting their opinions and values will be faced with statements that may puzzle, that seem to make no sense, that are ambiguous, that provoke, that exasperate, and that may even infuriate. Yet, if students are to become more reflective in what they think and say, teachers cannot respond judgmentally, lest the opportunity for examination be lost, and students put on the defensive, only to find their belief positions more deeply entrenched.

If searching for intelligent meaning and critical examination is the goal, teachers' nonjudgmental responses and questions that call for more thoughtful reflection are the better strategies. Learning to let go of responses that judge, despite the emotional tug of some of students' statements, is not easy, but it is key to the kind of interactive dialogue that is important in bringing students' beliefs under more critical examination. Underlying this is the teacher's respect for students and for their ideas—no matter how absurd, or wrong-headed, or patently false they seem—for without the teacher's respect, any attempts to engage them in an interactive dialogue in which their ideas are brought to critical examination are less than useless.

In some of the earlier chapters of this book, a few examples of questions and responses have been offered to show how they encourage students' examination of their ideas in response to some of the thinking tasks. In this chapter, a more detailed discussion is presented, demonstrating the kinds of responses and questions that are an important facet of "teaching for thinking."

Students' work on the curriculum tasks that derive from the thinking operations is one dimension of what is needed to cultivate students' more intelligent habits of mind. A second, and equally important, dimension is the way in which teachers further that examination through the use of reflective responses and higher-order questions.

SCENES FROM THE CLASSROOM

One of the best ways in which teachers may learn about the kind of interactive dialogue that respectfully engages students and brings their ideas under critical examination is by observing experienced teachers in the act of "discussion teaching." Failing that, a second strategy is to study the interactive dialogue through a series of scripts that are representative of that kind of discussion. In the scripts that follow, it is important to be aware of the teacher's absence of judgment, the kinds of reflective responses used, and the nature and use of higher-order questions—all combining to bring students' ideas under critical examination. Important too is the "tone" of teachers' responses and the "rhythm" of the interactive dialogue.

And finally, it should be noted that these interactive discussions do not lead, immediately, to a reconstruction of beliefs or ideas. What they do is plant the seeds, clarify the thought processes, and stir up discrepant notions for the student to continue to reflect on, which much later emerge as newly formed and better substantiated ideas.

Scenario A: A group of grade 7 students is observing a jar of locusts as part of their ongoing studies of insect life.

Teacher: What observations did you make about these locusts?

Liam: This is weird. Their eyes are right here (points).

Teacher: Their eyes are on the sides of their heads.

Liam: Yeah. That's strange.

Teacher: That seems strange to you. Maybe you're suggesting they should be in a different place.

Liam: They should be in front. But they're not.

Teacher: I see. You're suggesting that there may be something different in how the eyes of this insect are placed.

Liam: So that they can see in front and in back of them.

Teacher: Insects can see in front and in back of them?

Liam: Yes, I guess.

Teacher: Hmm. I see. Thanks for that, Liam. I wonder what these things are for? Does anyone have any ideas about them? (Points to antennae)

Georgina: I think they're feelers. Maybe they are antlers.

Teacher: You think they may be feelers or antlers.

Georgina: Yeah, feelers.

Teacher: Feelers, but not antlers.

Georgina: Yeah. Not antlers.

Teacher: Do you have any ideas about what they may be for?

Laura: Well they're to feel.

Teacher: Can you say a little more about that, Laura?

Laura: To feel their way around, when they can't see too well.

Teacher: Liam suggested that with the way their eyes are positioned, they can see in front and back. And now, Laura, you're suggesting that the antennae are for feeling their way around when they can't see. How do you explain that?

Laura: I don't know. I'm just guessing.

Teacher: You're guessing, but you don't know for sure. Thanks, Laura.

Scenario B: Transcript of grade 12 students discussing the ways in which voters make choices about candidates running for elective office after having read a news article in a local paper that described the ways in which delegates assembled to elect the new leader of British Columbia's Social Credit party made their choice.

Teacher: What are your views about how voters choose the best candidate?

June: I think the media influences our opinions. We tend to go for the candidate that has the most media appeal.

Teacher: Say a little more about that, June, about how that works.

June: I think the media plays a big role in presenting a candidate favorably. You know, how he or she appears on the screen, what clothes are worn, how the person smiles, or doesn't smile. These are the factors that seem to count and, of course, it depends on which channel you are watching because different channels, that support their own candidates, will present the best or the worst features of that candidate. And never mind what the person is talking about.

Teacher: You believe that what the person looks like is more important to voters than what that person is saying. And different media sources will emphasize those negative or positive characteristics.

June: I think it's sad but true. People don't listen. They are just looking.

Ruben: I don't agree. In my family, we discuss the issues. The issues are important to us. We don't make decisions based on whether the guy is wearing a $2,000 suit or if he's got a $200 haircut.

Teacher: In your family, it's the issues that count. Appearance is not an issue for you and your folks. To what extent do you consider your family to be typical, Ruben?

Ruben: I can't say for sure. I hope that we are typical, but I'm afraid that June may have a point. Other families may go for surface issues.

Teacher: You're not sure how typical your family is, but you are guessing that for other families, appearances might enter heavily into decision making.

Shawana: I think there's more to it than just issues. I think it's how people interpret what the issues are. I'm not sure that people are really interested in the issues. They are more interested in the slogans that represent the issues.

Teacher: Slogans pass as issues? How does that work?

Shawana: Well, for example, the free trade issue. I mean, how many people have gone deeply into the issue of free trade, and read all the literature? How many are just out there with their picket signs, like "down with free trade?" I think people just sign onto an issue without really considering what's behind it.

Teacher: People make choices about candidates based on incomplete knowledge of the issues. They are persuaded by slogans that don't tell the whole story.

Shawana: Yeah. There's a lot of media hype and then the issue gets reduced to its simplest terms. Like, remember George Bush, "No new taxes"? That's an example of signing onto a hot issue, without fully understanding its implications.

Teacher: The candidates and the media are guilty of provoking voters' passions with these slogans. Voters then tend to vote with their emotions instead of with their intelligence? Have I gone too far in making an interpretation of what you have said?

Shawana: No, you haven't. That's just what I mean.

Scenario C: The Pathway Junior Secondary School. Mr. Clavell is teaching science to his grade 8 class. The lesson is Squids. The teacher purchased two kilograms of squids for $5.50 in the local Chinese market. He brought them into the classroom and gave them out, one squid for each pair of students. With newspapers protecting their desks and a good supply of paper towels, the pupils were instructed to make some observations of the squids. They used some dissecting tools and laid out the parts of the animal. With magnifying glasses, they were able to study individual, small parts of the structure. This activity lasted for about thirty minutes, after which the teacher gathered the students for a discussion of what they had observed.

Teacher: So tell me, what observations did you make about squids?

Farley: Well, the most obvious was that there were these tentacles at the tail part of the squid.

Teacher: You found some tentacles, and you say that this was obvious to see. And you found them at the tail part of the squid.

Farley: Yeah.

Teacher: You have some reason to believe that the tentacles are found at the tail?

Farley: Well, I'm just assuming that that's true. 'Cause they are like tails, and so they should be at the tail.

Teacher: You're not certain. But because the tentacles look like tails, they would be at the tail part of the squid.

Carol: I disagree. I found what looks like a mouth, right in the center of the area where the tentacles are.

Teacher: So Carol, you and Farley have some different theories about where the tentacles are found. You see them at the head of the squid, with a mouth in the center.

Carol: That's odd. If they are like tails, then what's the mouth doing there?

Teacher: It seems odd to you. The mouth and the tentacles in the same region.

Stan: I have a theory about it. The tentacles, I think, it's how the squid moves. Don't they propel themselves using their tentacles? Like feet? The feet are in the head? I know that sounds peculiar.

Teacher: You have a theory, but it sounds a little strange to you. Their tentacles are like feet since they are used to propel them, but the mouth is there, among those tentacles. And that seems to be the head of the squid.

Stan: Yes. It's peculiar.

Teacher: Perhaps you want to think about that for a bit? Anyone else want to say anything more about the tentacles, or about the mouth?

Jean: It has no shell. But it's got this little piece of something, that's kinda like a bone but soft, inside.

Teacher: No shell, but something inside, that is almost like a bone, but soft. Like cartilage.

Jean: Yes, cartilage. But no skeleton inside.

Teacher: You didn't find a skeleton. So they are invertebrate? Is that what you are saying?

Jean: Yeah.

Teacher: I wonder what you might make out of this—they are classified, bio-logically, as cephalopods. How does that explain the "feet in the head" theory of Stan's?

Scenario D: The grade 4 teacher had read a story about life in a Pueblo village in the late eighteenth century, and she asked the students to talk about their observations of that village life.

Teacher: Yesterday I read a story to you about life among the Pueblo Indians long ago. I wonder what observations you were able to make about the way they lived. What are your ideas? Yes, Helen?

Helen: They got their food by hunting.

Teacher: One way they had of getting food was by hunting.

Helen: Yeah. They got rabbits.

Teacher: So rabbits were an important source of meat for the Pueblos.

Helen: Yeah.

Teacher: I wonder why they didn't just go to the supermarket.

(Pupils giggle)

Teacher: That sounds a little funny to you.

Melvin: They didn't have supermarkets in those days.

Teacher: No supermarkets, eh? Hmmm, I wonder how people could get along without a supermarket where you can shop and get anything you need.

Sarah: I think it just means, like, you have to grow your own. Like you have to grow your own vegetables and stuff.

Teacher: So without a market, you would need to grow your own food. And the Pueblos did this?

Sarah: Yeah. They grew corn and stuff.

Teacher: So they had to rely on their skills as farmers in order to get their food.

Frank: Well, they did other things, like collect berries. I don't think they grew the berries but they just went out there and picked them off the bushes.

Teacher: Another way of getting food was by gathering what was already grow-ing. There were some fruits that they didn't have to plant themselves.

(Students voice their agreement)

Teacher: I guess there's a big difference in your life if you have to depend on hunting, planting and gathering your own food, rather than just getting what you need at the local market. I wonder how that could affect your life? Do you have any ideas about it?

THE INTERACTIVE DIALOGUE

Teachers who have studied the use of responses and questions that promote students' further examination of their ideas, issues, and beliefs have pointed to several skills which they use, in concert, to bring students' thinking under further examination. These are not all the skills teachers use, but to those who use this kind of discussion teaching, they seem to be the ones considered important. In effective discussions, the teacher:

- Listens, attends, and apprehends what the student is saying
- Comprehends the statement the student is making
- Selects, from a range of options, the type of response to be made, with full appreciation that different responses have different cognitive and affective effects
- Chooses questions that put the student's ideas under examination
- Asks questions that promote cognitive dissonance

These basic principles of the interactive dialogue are discussed in more detail below. However, what is a necessary condition is the teacher's obvious show of respect for what the student is saying—no matter how odd, or bizarre, or wrong-headed it seems—for without that respect, there is little chance that the student will be able to consider and reconsider any idea that is discrepant with his or her original idea. Part of that showing of respect is the teacher's ability to refrain from making any kind of judgment about the student's statement, even avoiding the seemingly innocuous, "That's interesting."

- **Listening, attending, and apprehending** what the student is saying are evidenced in the teacher's behavior. Turning full attention to the student, in body language, face, and eyes, the teacher communicates, "I hear you. I am listening to what you have to say." Attending means more than just hearing the words. It includes observing all behavioral clues as the words are being spoken. Listening, attending, and apprehending require a full and conscious effort to tune in to the student's idea.
- **Comprehending the student's meaning** is greatly helped by the teacher's ability to listen, to attend, and to apprehend what the student is saying. Using both visual and auditory cues the teacher is able to discern the surface and below-the-surface meanings. A moment of reflection—what IS the student saying?—enables the teacher to process and then to understand. One strategy that some teachers use to understand is to "say back" what the teacher has heard the student saying and to ask, "I'm going to try to say back what you have told me and you can tell me whether I have understood you correctly." Or even, "Would you help me to understand by telling me again what you mean?"

- In **selecting a response to the idea** the student is presenting, the teacher has a range of options, all of which encourage student's examination of his or her original idea. Responses that should be avoided are those which agree or disagree, those which are judgmental, and those which provide information, or offer the teacher's ideas, as they are not helpful in that further examination, but tend, rather, to close down the student's thinking. Responses that call for further examination include the following:

  - Saying the idea back to the student in some new way
  - Paraphrasing the idea
  - Interpreting the idea
  - Asking for more information

  Any of these types of responses are respectful of the student and the ideas, and will make it safe for the student to explore further.
- **Responses that call for analysis of the student's idea** are more challenging than those "basic" responses that simply mirror the student's statement. These kinds of responses require deeper examination on the student's part and go beyond surface observations. Such responses include the following:

  - A request that examples be given
  - A query as to whether assumptions are being made
  - A query as to whether alternatives have been considered
  - A request that comparisons be made
  - A request for supporting data
  - A query as to where the idea came from

  The above suggestions are not an exhaustive list of what may be asked but give an idea about the kinds of questions that may be raised in asking students to dig deeper into what they are saying, to try to puzzle out the frame of reference for where the ideas came from and how substantive they are.
- **Questions that challenge and that promote cognitive dissonance** are the most demanding of the students and of their ideas. They require students to extend their thinking, to take data and reconfigure them into new frameworks, and to come up with new ideas—so that something new and different emerges from the discussion. These kinds of challenging responses include asking that:

  - Hypotheses be generated
  - Data be interpreted
  - Principles be applied to new situations
  - Evaluations be made and criteria be identified
  - Predictions be made about what is possible
  - Plans of action be originated

• Decisions be made and their consequences examined

Again, this is not an exhaustive list of what may be asked so that students may be challenged about what they think and what they believe, but they provide examples of the kinds of questions that do provoke cognitive dissonance and call students' ideas into question.

It is often the case that teachers who challenge students' statements frequently fall back on the "why?" question. This question is arguably the most frequently heard in classrooms in the form, "Why do you think so?" Or sometimes, "Why or why not?" This question is intended as a challenge, and its purpose is to have the student defend an idea, a principle, or a proposition with data.

However, teachers who are habituated to interactive classroom dialogues ordinarily shun the use of "why" questions, since experience has taught them that they are too confrontational and too challenging to be productive. Moreover, "why" covers a vast amount of territory, which can only be partially answered in a student response. It is suggested then that "why" questions be scrapped in favor of "what" questions. For example:

• What reasons do you have for those suggestions?
• What data support your ideas?
• What examples can you give?

SOME FINAL WORDS

There is much more to the art of discussion teaching than merely making interrogative demands. If students are to benefit from the teacher's use of questions that bring that student's ideas under the light of intelligent scrutiny, not only must the questions be sensitively framed, respectful, articulate, and inviting, they must also be conceptualized to allow the student's examination to get at the heart of the real issues.

Finding the "right" question—the one with the capacity to rattle the student's closed-minded view—is one way of piercing dogmatic thinking. If the mind can be envisioned as a giant cognitive jigsaw puzzle, with trillions of connecting pieces that make patterns of pictures that shape thinking (Snygg 1966), the "irritating" question becomes like a grain of sand in an oyster shell, a troublesome, prickly thing that jars already framed cognitive patterns and weasels its way into the interstices between the pieces, looking for someplace to fit. The mind must work to free itself from such a cognitive burden.

Orchestrating all the strands of an interactive dialogue with students is a high-level professional undertaking. For the teacher new to these demands, a caution: these skills are not mastered in a day. Some teachers devote a lifetime to honing them. Like other important teaching skills, this is learned more on the job than in any preparatory program.

But given these suggestions, teachers who follow them will quickly see the effects on student thinking and processing and that, in itself, is a substantial reward for such an undertaking.

Chapter 17

Evaluating Students' Work

The tradition in public schools is to evaluate students work by pointing out what is correct and what is in error. Ignoring work that is done online, which is a special category, "pencil-and-paper" tasks are usually marked with a red pencil, or pen, and the process includes totaling up the rights and wrongs that lead to a mark that is positioned at the top of the page. This kind of assessment is done on workbook exercises, on homework, and, of course, on tests. Marks may appear in either letter or number form and, in that way, students are ranked according to the quality of their performance.

When it comes to work on essays in English or in social studies, for example, the traditional process is to point out spelling, grammatical, or punctuation errors, and perhaps even inconsistencies in argument or in narrative form. More careful attention to narrative or essay writing searches out what has been elegantly stated, what is blatantly false, what needs reconsideration, and the student may be asked to consult with the teacher for more information or for specific help.

In these types of activities, a "mark" is usually awarded for the quality of the work—and a teacher's experience with many students, over the years, will give him or her a "narrative ear" for the kind of work that is good, not so good, or perhaps far above average, and the student's mark will reflect that appraisal.

In this process, in which students are immersed for all of their school lives, they learn that it is the teacher's job to assess and rate them, as they would eggs going to market. Students become habituated to this kind of assessment, and many of them believe that those assessments of their performance and worth are true.

Given the history and the traditional ways of marking and evaluating students' work, what is being proposed in these pages may appeal revolutionary.

However, the suggestions that follow are in keeping with the overall design and aims of building students' intelligent habits of mind. This is not to say that teachers should abandon their traditional assessment procedures. It is to say, however, that in evaluating and assessing students' work on teaching for thinking activities, they are singularly inappropriate.

If the goal of these activities is to raise students' awareness of the quality of their thinking, provide them with the organizers that enable them to discern what needs further examination, and help them build from the teacher's feedback, then more appropriate strategies that are in accord with the goals, are suggested.

ASSESSING STUDENTS' WORK

There are several factors that teachers consider in assessing students' work on thinking tasks. One is the nature and quality of the student's accurate use of data to inform any analysis being made on the task. Another is the depth of awareness of the analysis. A third is the extent to which the student has "profitably used" the information. Not the least is the student's ability to remain free from making unwarranted assumptions, in drawing conclusions that go beyond the data, in differentiating what is fact and what is false.

A student who is having difficulty with academic work, or is emotionally troubled, or has manifested a lack of ability to think clearly may perform at a lower level than one who is successful in almost every academic endeavor. Teachers are aware that levels of performance for students may be different, yet—and this is a *sine qua non*—it is vital that teachers' expectations do not diminish students, for to expect less is demeaning and harmful. So it is on this see-saw of a balance beam that teachers make their judgments.

There is a huge difference, too, in the ways in which feedback is offered to students. In assessing work on thinking tasks, comments that are punitive or harshly critical are not only hurtful, but also counterproductive to the goals. They are, first of all, disrespectful, and second, do not serve the purpose of promoting intelligent habits of mind. In fact, such comments may be so defeating that they impact on a students' relationship with the teacher. So learning to give critical feedback in respectful ways is another important element in the kind of comments that are given on students' work.

Examples of how these strategies are applied on students' activities may give clearer ideas of how this is done. In the overall, the kind and quality of feedback on students' work is not only a key feature of furthering their intelligent habits of mind, but it is also a significant way of enabling them to take the next steps in becoming more rational, more reflective, more thoughtful, more mature, and wiser in the way they access and interpret information.

Example A

The grade 7 students were studying the people, civilization, and culture of Ancient Egypt and were given the assignment of examining how wind-powered ships made a difference to their lives, in terms of the benefits they brought. The teacher considered this to be an example of how students might use data from their textbooks to suggest hypotheses about the importance of this mode of transportation.

Javier used his textbook to gather data for his work and produced the following paper:

Ships that were powered by the wind helped them to travel. Because they didn't have motors in those days. They could use the ships to fish for food, and to get from place to place. They could grow crops and vegetables and grapes for wine. They could use grain to make bread. They had a lot of animals too.

Teacher's feedback:

Hi, Javier. You have pointed to an important way in which wind-powered ships helped people to get around in the early days of the Ancient Egyptian civilization. You also mentioned that wind-powered ships could help them fish for food, since in those early days they had no motors.

I'm wondering, however, if growing crops and vegetables depended on the wind-powered ships and perhaps you could help to explain this more? I'm wondering too how using grain to make bread depended on wind-powered ships? Can you help to explain this more?

Perhaps you can think of some other important ways in which the use of wind-powered ships benefited the Ancient Egyptians?

Example B

The grade 3 students were studying seeds and plants and were given the task of comparing the illustrations of two plants, one that had been watered and one that was lacking in hydration.

Rajendra wrote the following:

One plant is growing nice and tall. It is full of leaves and the leaves are all green. It looks so happy to me. Like someone has taken good care of it and gave it food and lots of water.

One plant looks like it is dying. The leaves are all brown and they are falling off. It looks so sad to me like no one has taken care of it and given it food or water.

The plants are the same kind, but one is good and the other is dying.

Teacher's feedback:

Hi, Rajendra. You studied the two plants and you saw that one was a healthy-looking plant and the other looked like it was dying. You believe that the healthy plant has been given food and water and that is why it is healthy. You believe that the plant that is dying did not get any food or water. How can you know that is true? What are your ideas?

Example C

The grade 6 students were reading Harry Potter and the teacher asked them to suggest some hypotheses for the enormous success of that series of books. May Le wrote,

> *Maybe it's because the stories are so good.*
> *Maybe it's because kids like us like to read about that kind of stuff.*
> *Maybe it's because the writing is so good.*
> *Maybe it's because the characters are so interesting.*
> *Maybe it's because it's better than other books.*
> *That's all I can think of now.*

Teacher's feedback:

Hi, May Le: You suggested a few hypotheses to explain why you believe the Harry Potter books are so popular. Perhaps it is because the stories are so interesting and the writing is so good? Maybe it's because the characters are interesting? I'm wondering, what makes an interesting character? Do you have any ideas about that?

If you were to describe an "interesting character," what would be some of the features of that character?

Example D

The grade 8 students were studying the experiments of Galileo that led to his being investigated by the Roman Inquisition in 1615, and with his life in peril, he recanted his scientific conclusions that the earth moved around the sun.

The teacher asked them to suggest hypotheses for the reasons the authorities were not only hostile to his scientific discoveries, but were fearful of what he had found.

Ariel wrote,

> *It was heresy to go against the church in those days. The church dictated the law*
> *and if you went against the church teachings, you could be burned as a witch,*

or sent to prison. I don't know why the church was so closed minded and why they were rejecting of science.

Teacher's feedback:

Hi, Ariel. You are hypothesizing that it was the church in those times that made the laws and was in authority. To go against them was like breaking the law today, is that what you mean? And if you went against the church, you had to pay a great penalty, perhaps your life was at stake. You can't figure out why the church in those days was so set in their ways as to not be open to science. Do you think it had anything to do with the way they wanted to control what people believed and what they thought? What do you think?

Example E

The grade 10 students were studying the Civil Rights Act of 1964 in the United States that prohibited discrimination based on race, color, religion, sex, or national origin. It prohibited unequal application of voter registration requirements, racial segregation in schools, employment, and public accommodations.

The teacher asked the students to suggest hypotheses to explain why it took so long for the United States to pass legislation outlawing racial discrimination after President Lincoln signed the Emancipation Proclamation.

Selena wrote,

I think it's because so many people have prejudice against people of color. I think it's because people were scared of having black children in their schools.
I think it's because they wanted to keep black people down so they could pay them less for more work. I think the Congress didn't want to pass the law because there were too many southern senators who were racists.

Teacher's feedback:

Thank you for your thoughtful comments in your hypotheses, Selena. I see you have suggested that some of the reasons for the long delay in passing the Civil Rights legislation has to do with lingering racist feelings among many white people. You also point to some economic benefits of keeping black people in lower-level jobs and with lower pay. I wonder if you have considered where racist feelings come from and how it's possible that they continue to exist in our country? What are your ideas?

Example F

As a problem-solving and decision-making task, the teacher assigned the grade 11 students the activity of designing an immigration law that would identify what groups, if any, should be given preference for immigrating to Canada. They were asked how they would decide about the groups to be given least preference. They were also asked to state how they made these determinations.

The students at first worked in small groups to gather data, to consult, and to create suggestions and plans. Then, they worked individually to present their own ideas.

Craig wrote,

I think that in the past the Canadian government has been far too liberal in allowing immigration of all people to enter Canada, without consideration for the people who have been here first. Too much immigration causes problems for those who are here. They must be looked after, taught the new language, find jobs, houses, and schools. They will work for less money and take jobs away from Canadians. I think that Canada should stop being so open door to everyone and keep immigration small. Other countries should take their share of immigrants. We should not be the only ones to take them in.

Teacher's response to Craig's paper:

Hi, Craig. I see that you have some strong opinions about keeping the doors to Canada open to any new immigrants. You believe that allowing large numbers of immigrants to enter Canada will impact on jobs and on the economy for Canadians. I'm wondering how, in the past, immigration has hurt or benefitted Canada? What do the data in your textbooks say about that? My other thought is to ask you about people whose lives are in jeopardy because of what is going on in their own countries. What would be your ideas about making any concessions for them coming into Canada?

The above examples do not represent the be-all and end-all of the kinds of comments that teachers make in feedback to students' work on thinking tasks. But they do give some ideas of how teachers respond to the type and quality of student thinking and how they also provide some next steps for their further consideration. In all of the above, teachers will note that no comment is punitive or disrespectful and that students' ideas are "heard" and used as working material for their further thought.

One final note must be added about the kinds of comments teachers make on thinking tasks. It is immediately seen that to create such comments takes more teacher time on task than merely placing "Xs" next to incorrect items. While that is true, teachers who have used these forms of feedback to students have claimed that the interest that students' responses generate more than compensates for the extra time needed to evaluate their work.

BUT IS IT WORKING?

Teachers who have embarked on a program that puts emphasis on higher-order thinking will want to ensure that their program has been effective. Are their students learning to process data more intelligently? Are students becoming more informed? Are they seen to be developing more intelligent habits of mind? Teachers will want to know this for themselves, for students, for parents, and for administrators. They will want to know not only *that* students are learning, but also *what* they are learning and *how well* it has been learned.

One way in which teachers will know this is by the nature of students' responses on their curriculum tasks. With experience in thinking activities that are derived from the thinking operations, students should, over time, manifest more critical mindedness in their responses. Their responses will become more thoughtful, more analytical, and more free from unwarranted assumptions and conclusions that go far beyond the data.

Another way in which students will reveal their growth in using more intelligent habits of mind will be seen in their behavior.

A group of teachers working together suggested some basic standards of behavior for making such behavioral observations of students as they grow in their thinking skills (Adam et al. 2000). In other words, students who have benefited from long-term work with thinking should exhibit their thoughtfulness in at least some of the following ways:

- Is able to identify the big ideas of the essay, plot, frame of reference, story, editorial, and broadcast—in other words, extract meaning from data accurately
  - Is tolerant for the ideas and opinions of others
  - Is able to differentiate between opinion and fact; between assumptions and fact
  - Shows tolerance for contrary data
  - Can give examples to support ideas
  - Can make intelligent interpretations of data
  - Is original, inventive, and creative in his or her work
  - Has a higher tolerance for ambiguity
  - Can see problems and issues through a larger perspective
  - Is able to collect and organize data intelligently
  - Is able to extract and record information accurately
  - Considers "thinking" a useful tool in solving problems and making decisions

Another way of using student behavior to observe improved higher-order thinking is by using Raths's (1986) thinking-related behaviors as a template. He suggested that students who developed more intelligent habits of mind would reveal that growth in the reduction of their "thinking-related behaviors," those behaviors symptomatic of dysfunctional or limited habits of thinking. In short, if students were seen to behave less frequently and less extremely in the following ways, that would be one important indicator of growth in their thinking abilities:

- *Impulsiveness*: These students respond "without thinking. They "leap to conclusions" before the data are in. They seem to react on the spur of the moment without thought.
- *Overdependence on the teacher or other adult authority*: These students seem to need help at every step of the way. They don't seem to be able to function on their own. They don't seem to be able to "think for themselves."
- *Inability to connect means with ends*: These students seem unable to see the relationship between process and product. They are unable to make a connection between what they are doing and the results of their activities.
- *Missing the meaning*: These students "don't seem to get it." If they are asked to give a summary of a story, or an article, or a broadcast, they are unable to find the meaning, and, rather than a summary, would repeat the whole of it in great detail. They are unable to find "the big ideas" in what is read, seen, or heard.
- *Dogmatic, overly assertive behavior*: These students seem unable to see beyond their own deeply entrenched positions. Their positions are often not supported by any data but come from their own experience or belief positions. They are dogmatic and assertive where the evidence is lacking; they are sure when thoughtful people entertain doubt. They have a low tolerance for the ideas and views of others, so wedded are they to their own "truths."
- *Rigidity, inflexibility of behavior*: These students seem to have a hard time with ideas, strategies, and systems that are new. They are locked into routines and strategies that are familiar to them. They act out of habit, rather than out of a consideration of what the situation requires. There is a resistance to new ideas, new materials, new ways of doing things, and new situations. There is a preference for what is old and what has worked for them in the past.
- *Lack of confidence in one's own thinking*: These students almost never volunteer ideas of their own. Underlying that may be the fear that an idea must be absolutely correct if it is going to be voiced, that thoughts must be absolutely true in order for them to be spoken. There is timidity about these students, a lack of confidence in self and in their ideas.

- *Unwillingness to think*: These students have made a value judgment against thinking. They are the "lesson learners" of the classroom. They believe that it is the teacher's job to do the thinking and their job is to follow instructions and get the "right answers" that are called for in the text. They are resistant to change and difficult to work with in a classroom where the emphasis is on thinking.

Once other possible causative factors such as emotional and physical health problems have been ruled out, teachers might safely proceed on the assumption that these types of behaviors are, indeed, symptoms associated with dysfunctional thinking. Much research has been done to indicate that a major reduction in these counterproductive patterns of behavior is seen in after a long-term program where the emphasis is on promoting more intelligent habits of mind (Raths 1986). Such reduction in these "thinking-related behaviors" would be an important indicator of students' growth as thinkers.

USING SELF-ASSESSMENTS

Teachers at both elementary and secondary school levels have used self-assessment as a tool for evaluating student growth and progress in a program that emphasizes higher-order thinking. And these teachers who have used various self-assessment tools have all indicated their faith in the abilities of their students to make honest and self-aware evaluations of their work on thinking tasks. Many teachers have devised their own tools and one of these is offered below, as one example of what can be asked of students when they are assessing their own work. It has been adapted from the work of Adams et al. (2000) with permission from the authors, and teachers are permitted to duplicate these materials for their own classroom use.

PROFILES OF STUDENT BEHAVIORS

Directions:

In this self-evaluation exercise, there are twenty Profiles of Student Behavior. Each profile presents a brief sketch that shows how people learn and how they think. Your job is to decide how your behavior "matches" what is written in that profile sketch. In other words, how do you see your behavior as representative of the description in the profile. You are the one who makes that decision. Try to decide how your behavior "fits" the profile in general, rather than on a single day. Add any comments you'd care to make in the space below the profile.

Rate it 1 if you believe your behavior matches the description almost all of the
    time.
Rate it 2 if you believe your behavior matches the description most of the time.
Rate it 3 if you believe your behavior matches the description some of the time.
Rate it 4 if you believe your behavior matches the description almost none of
    the time.

I. INTELLECTUAL DEVELOPMENT

1. Quality of thinking

1.1 Sees the big idea

When you read about or listen to an article, a story, an essay, or a news
broadcast, you are able to understand the important ideas. When you present
arguments or points of view, you are clear about the important issues.

                                                        Rating_____

Comments:

1.2 Shows tolerance for the ideas and opinions of others

You are open to what other people think. You respect their views even if they
disagree with yours. You listen closely to other people's point of view and
respond to their ideas in a thoughtful and respectful way.

                                                        Rating_____

Comments:

1.3 Knows the difference between facts, opinions, and assumptions

You understand the difference between facts, assumptions, and opinions.
When you present information to support your arguments, you are able to pres-
ent your facts knowledgeably and your assumptions and opinions with caution.
You let people know that you are stating your opinions when you do so.

                                                        Rating_____

Comments:

1.4 Shows tolerance for contrary data

Even though you may believe something very strongly, you are usually able
to consider different points of view. When you are faced with information

that is different from what you believe, you examine it thoughtfully and carefully to see how it fits in with your thinking.

Rating_____

Comments:

1.5 Can give examples to support ideas

When you are asked to provide examples to support your arguments, you are able to do so without difficulty. What's more, the examples you choose are clearly related to what you have been saying.

Rating_____

Comments:

1.6 Can make intelligent interpretations of data

You are able to understand what you have heard, or observed, or read, and you are able to communicate that understanding to others. What's more, you are cautious about drawing conclusions about what you have heard or seen when there is insufficient evidence.

Rating_____

Comments:

1.7 Demonstrates originality, creativity, and inventiveness in written work

You are able to go beyond what is ordinary and create new ideas and products. You are original and inventive and what comes out of your mind is fresh, new, and imaginative. You are able to take risks and push yourself to the limits of creativity.

Rating_____

Comments:

1.8 Demonstrates awareness that the ability to think is an important way to solve problems and make decisions

You value thinking as a way of solving problems and as a way of making decisions. You want to think for yourself and you want to think your own ideas. You are independent and view thinking as a tool to enrich your life.

                                                                    Rating_____

Comments:

II. SKILLS

2. Communication of Ideas

2.1 Written work is an example of the quality of thinking

Your written ideas are presented clearly and are based on many different sources of information including facts, observations, details, and statistics. You are able to provide examples that clarify what you mean. Your writing is well organized. You use well-constructed sentences and give thought to spelling, punctuation, and capitalization. You are able to communicate your ideas in a way that is interesting to the reader.

                                                                    Rating_____

Comments:

2.2 Oral presentations are examples of the quality of thinking

When you make an oral presentation, your language is clear and you support your ideas with data. Your ideas are interesting and it is easy for others to understand what you are saying. When you argue your point of view, you make sense.

                                                                    Rating_____

Comments:

3. Research Skills

3.1 Is able to collect and organize information in a coherent way

You are able to locate and gather data from many sources. When you use the information you have collected in your oral or written work, it is organized in a way that makes sense and focuses on the important issues. You use the information you collect to examine different sides of an issue and draw your conclusions based on this balanced examination.

Rating_____

Comments:

3.2 Is able to extract and record information accurately

When you research a topic, you use a variety of sources and you are able to gather the information that zeroes in on the important issues. You don't have much difficulty knowing what is important and what may be left out. You are able to record the information you have gathered in a way that makes sense.

Rating_____

Comments:

4. *Interpersonal Skills*

4.1 Is able to listen and attend thoughtfully to the ideas of others

In group discussions, you are able to listen carefully to the ideas of others and hear what they are saying. The way you respond to other students lets them know that you have heard them and understood what they have said.

Rating_____

Comments:

4.2 Contributes to the facilitation of group discussion

When working in a group, you listen carefully to the ideas of other students even if the ideas expressed do not agree with your own. It's easy for you to be respectful of the ideas of others and to show that respect in your group discussions. You take an active part in making sure that the group discussions are productive and that is as important to you as getting out your own ideas.

Rating_____

Comments:

III. ATTITUDES

5. Personal Perspectives

5.1 Has a positive outlook

You see problems as challenges. When faced with a problem, you feel confident in your ability to solve it. You like to challenge yourself and even when you are not successful in solving a problem, you are able to keep your confidence as a problem solver.

Rating_____

Comments:

5.2 Has a high tolerance for ambiguity

When you are faced with conflicting information, you are patient and you are not compelled to decide until better information is available. When you face a situation that appears to be neither right nor wrong, that does not make you uncomfortable. You are comfortable even when the answers have not been found.

Rating_____

Comments:

5.3 Has a global perspective

When you examine an issue, you are able to see how it affects other people in your school, community, or city. You realize how your school and your community are related to the whole world, and you appreciate all people as part of a world community.

Rating_____

Comments:

6. Beliefs and Values

6.1 Your beliefs inform your behavior

You think about what you believe and you are really clear about what is important to you. There is a clear connection between what you believe and how you act. Your actions over time are a clear reflection of your values.

Rating_____

Comments:

7. *Self-Evaluation*

7.1 Is open to self-evaluation

You welcome the chance to evaluate your own work. You see self-evaluation as a chance to learn more about yourself, as an opportunity to examine your strengths and weaknesses, and determine where more work is needed. You are not afraid to be honest in owning up to where you are having trouble. This ability to look at yourself honestly allows you to be more open to learning.

Rating_____

Comments:

7.2 Shows skill and insight in self-evaluation

You are able to look at your own work critically. You are thoughtful in examining your work and you can see your strengths and weaknesses realistically. You can recognize where you need help and you are able to ask for that help as part of the process of learning. You are not defensive about owning up to your need to improve.

Rating_____

Comments:

SCENES FROM THE CLASSROOM

The sixth-grade class that had been immersed all year in a program that emphasized higher-order thinking was visited, in June, by a group of college students who were training to become teachers. The college students were given an opportunity to question the sixth graders about their experiences in the program, and one asked how, given all the freedoms that they had enjoyed during this last year of elementary school, would they be able to adjust to a departmentalized junior high school.

Eddie, who was initially a boy that had been identified as one with some observable symptoms of dysfunctional thinking behaviors, volunteered to say:

> *This type of sixth grade program has taught us to have self-discipline and to think for ourselves. I feel that I could face any kind of seventh grade and do a good job, because thinking for yourself teaches you how to handle any new situation.*

Chapter 18

The Teacher Is the Key

For those who look at teaching from outside the profession, it seems, on the surface, to be one of the easiest jobs in the world. After all, don't teachers get a short day, leaving school at 3:00 P.M.? Don't they get two months of summer holidays with pay?

Those who are not in the know don't realize that when teachers do, in fact, leave school in the midafternoon, they usually go home with a load of papers to mark, lesson plans to write, report cards to fill out, phone calls to make to parents, and other related professional tasks that take up not only the rest of the afternoon, but often extend into the early hours of the evening. That, however, is only a small part of the picture.

No one outside of the profession has a real idea of what a teacher's job entails, from the whirlwind of activity in the classroom, where some thirty-odd students, with energy unleashed, wrestle with the demands of learning, to the various and sundry professional tasks that teachers engage in, from moment to moment, thinking on their feet, managing discipline, addressing individual learning needs and problems, organizing curriculum, using appropriate teaching strategies, encouraging students to press forward when the going gets tough, and maintaining a positive attitude in the face of numerous student-related and administration-related problems. Sometimes, the burden of the tasks seems insurmountable.

A student teacher once complained to her mentor teacher about how hard the job of teaching was and how tired she felt at the end of each school day. The mentor teacher quipped, "If you wanted easier work, you should have become a nuclear physicist."

While the point is arguable, it is nonetheless true that few outside the profession have a full appreciation of the complexities of teaching and the arduous demands of the job.

Putting aside the myth that teaching is nothing more than standing in front of a group of students day after day, "explaining, demonstrating and showing how," and examining the multiple and complex aspects of what teachers actually do, one may begin to appreciate the true nature of a teacher's work.

For example, teachers are responsible for designing curriculum tasks for their students and for the preparation of original learning materials, selecting those that are particularly appropriate to students' individual learning needs. They are required to understand and deal effectively with the emotional, social, and intellectual problems that students present and give each the time and attention necessary so that improved learning may result. Teachers formatively and summatively evaluate students' learning, making diagnosis of performance on specific tasks, making thoughtful judgments about the whole of a student's performance over an interval of time, and reporting this in a comprehensible way to anxious parents.

Teachers work with large groups, with small groups, and with individuals, though the approach to each may require different interventions, different strategies, and different skills. They must be masters of teacher-student interactions, knowing when to respond facilitatively, when to question, what kinds of questions to ask, how to challenge students' thinking, and how and when to be judgmental and offer an opinion.

Teachers must be prepared to deal with students' behavior problems, knowing when and how to be tough and firm without diminishing a student's dignity and when to overlook the infractions. A teacher must know how to organize the classroom for instruction and how to make shifts in the organization so that the learning activity and organizational scheme are in concert—so that means and ends are congruent. A teacher is the composer, the orchestrator, and the conductor of the classroom symphony, if the students are to make beautiful music.

There are, of course, the demands of evaluation and assessment that occur daily on a wide variety of student papers, but also in oral and written reports to parents. What to write, how to write it, how to judge fairly and wisely, in a way that does not damage a student's self-esteem. There is both skill and art in this process and it is never easy.

On top of all of that, teachers also keep up with their professional development activities, reading what is current, attending workshops and professional day activities, and making intelligent distinctions about what new ideas are of real value.

It is no wonder that teachers are tired. The job is herculean.

As if the range and complexity of teachers' tasks were not enough, the job is further compounded by the fact that each task, each function that teachers carry out, requires that decisions be made. Every day and every minute of the day, teachers make decisions about curriculum: what to teach, how to organize the learning experience, what instructional approaches to use, what to give major emphasis to and what to exclude, and how and what to evaluate.

Teachers decide how to present material, determining how explicit to make explanations and how much to leave to inference. They decide how to supplement the standard curriculum, including selecting which materials to use. They decide how to evaluate student learning, which remedies are appropriate for students who are having difficulty, and what to report to parents. Teachers make decisions, perhaps implicitly through personal style, about classroom climate, group work, interpersonal relationships, discipline, and housekeeping.

They decide what professional in-service work to undertake in improving their own competence, and they make judgments about which new ideas are educationally sound and worth putting into practice. If the list sounds extensive, it barely scratches the surface. To further complicate matters, the decisions that teachers are required to make are rarely clear-cut. They involve considerable judgment and intuition as well as thoughtful consideration of data based on professional experience.

Such decision making is not only onerous, it is often full of tension, ambiguity, and risk. Most of these decisions are made alone, and it is often the case that they bear heavily on a teacher's psychological, physical, and emotional well-being.

Given all of that, now comes a textbook with a forceful argument that teachers undertake yet one more major task in their professional obligations—that is, to raise the level of thinking in all of their students, by designing curriculum activities that promote more intelligent habits of mind, tasking themselves with the burden of adapting new teacher-student classroom interactions that enable students to search for meaning in their curriculum work.

The argument is further made that the need for this work, in these times of 24/7 bombardment of information, the unexpurgated stream of rubbish from internet and social media, and the "alternate truths" that are disseminated by all and sundry, is more critical than ever before in our lifetimes. If a democracy, as Thomas Jefferson reminded us, rests on the foundation of an educated electorate—citizens who are able to understand the difference between fact and fantasy, who can use data to inform their decisions, then the case need not be made further. But in the end, it is and will always be the teachers' choice, guided by what they consider to be "what's important" in the education of their students.

The happy news is that it is not all one-sided. There is benefit to teachers who want to consider pursuing such a program, and that is seen in the observable results in student behavior. For there is no greater joy for a teacher to see students becoming empowered by their independence, their ability to reason, and their satisfaction in knowing that they have achieved something more than just silent acquiescence. In the end, the students will know that what their teacher has accomplished with them is to last them all of their lives.

And that's no small potatoes.

SCENES FROM THE CLASSROOM

A good teacher must have patients [sic] with the children and parents (at conferences) when they don't understand something. They must have good humor and laugh when something is funny, but they have to be strict sometimes. Thy must always have confidence in the children, show them and lead them on the right road to succes [sic]. They should be able to hold their temper and treat the child in a nice way. Not only do they teach from the book but in ways of making it fun to do it. They must know what work a child needs; otherwise, it makes it bad for him or her. They must always have love even for the bad ones.

Bibliography

Adam, Maureen, Rich Chambers, Steve Fukui, Joe Gluska, and Selma Wassermann. 2000. *Evaluation Materials for the Graduation Program*. Coquitlam, BC: Centennial Secondary School Case Study Project.

Aikin, Wilford M. 1942. *The Story of the Eight-Year Study*. New York: Harper & Brothers.

Anderson, Kurt. 2017. "How America Went Haywire." *The Atlantic*, September, 79.

Arkowitz, Hal, and Scott O. Lilienfeld. 2010. "Why Science Tells Us Not to Rely on Eyewitness Accounts." *Scientific American*, January 1.

Ashton-Warner, Sylvia. 1963, 1986. *Teacher*. New York: Simon & Schuster.

Bloom, Benjamin, ed. 1964. *Taxonomy of Educational Objectives. Handbook I: Cognitive Domain*. New York: David McKay.

Bracey, Gerald. 1998. "Minds of Our Own." *Phi Delta Kappan* 80, no. 4: 328–29.

Bruni, Frank. 2017. "I'm O.K.—You're Pure Evil." *New York Times*, June 19, 3.

Chang, Juju, and Jim Dubreuil. 2009. *Abducted by Aliens: Believers Tell Their Stories*. http://abcnews.go.com/Primetime/story?id=8330290.

Cheevers, Jack. 2013. *Act of War*. New York: NAL Caliber.

Cooper, Lane. 1917. *Louis Agassiz as a Teacher*. Ithaca, NY: Cornell University Press. Reprinted in C. Roland Christensen. 1987. *Teaching and the Case Method*. Boston, MA: Harvard Business School, 79–82.

Costa, Arthur. 1985. *Developing Minds: A Resource Book for Teaching Thinking*. Alexandria, VA: Association for Curriculum Development.

———. 2009. *Habits of Mind across the Curriculum*. Alexandria, VA: Association for Curriculum Development.

Dickerson, Caitlin. 2017. "How Fake News Turned a Small Town Upside Down." *New York Times*, October 1, 46–54.

Featherstone, Joseph. 2007. "Stories of the Eight-Year Study: Re-Examining Secondary Education in America." *Teachers College Record*, January 16.

Festinger, Leon. 1958. "The Motivating Effect of Cognitive Dissonance." In *The Cognitive Processes*, edited by Robert J. C. Harper, Charles C. Anderson, Clifford M. Christensen, and Stephen M. Hunka. Englewood, NJ: Prentice Hall.

Friedman, Thomas. 2017. "On Line and Scared." *New York Times*, January 11.

Gift, Jill. 1989. *Opportunities for Students to Make Decisions Affecting Their Learning in Four Elementary School Classrooms.* Unpublished master's thesis, Simon Fraser University, Faculty of Education, Vancouver, British Columbia.

Glasser, William. 1985. *Control Theory in the Classroom.* New York: HarperCollins.

Greenstone, Michael, and Adam Looney. 2011. "A Dozen Economic Facts about Innovation." *The Hamilton Project.* www.brookings.edu.

Horowitz, Jason. 2017. "In Italian Schools, Reading, Writing and Recognizing Fake News." *New York Times*, October 19.

Kahneman, Daniel. 2011. *Thinking Fast and Slow.* New York: Farrar, Straus and Giroux.

Kirsch, Adam. 2017. "The Hardest Lesson of a Liberal Democracy? How to Live with Critics." *New York Times Book Review*, June 18, 21.

Kolbert, Elizabeth. 2017. "Why Facts Don't Change Our Minds." *New Yorker*, February 27.

Loftus, E. F. 1980. "Impact of Expert Psychological Testimony on the Unreliability of Eyewitness Identification." *Journal of Applied Psychology* 65, no. 1: 9–15.

Mercier, Hugo, and Dan Sperber. 2017. *The Enigma of Reason.* Boston, MA: Harvard University Press.

Mutit, Linda. 1984. "Reflections on a Teaching Day." Excerpt from her personal journal and reprinted with permission.

Pogrow, Stanley. 2005. "HOTS Revisited: A Thinking Development Approach to Reducing the Learning Gap after Grade 3." *Phi Delta Kappan* 87, no. 1: 64–75.

Raths, Louis E., Merrill Harmin, and Sidney B. Simon. 1973. *Values and Teaching.* Columbus, OH: Charles Merrill.

Raths, Louis E., Selma Wassermann, Arthur Jonas, and Arnold Rothstein. 1966. *Teaching for Thinking: Theory and Application.* Columbus, OH: Charles Merrill.

———. 1986. *Teaching for Thinking: Theory and Application*, 2nd edition. New York: Teachers College Press.

Rogers, Carl. 2003. *On Becoming a Person*, 2nd edition. Boston, MA: Mariner Books.

Rokeach, Milton. 1960. *The Open and Closed Mind.* New York: Basic Books.

———. 1970. *Beliefs, Attitudes and Values.* San Francisco, CA: Jossey Bass.

Rutenberg, Jim. 2017. "The Disruption." *New York Times*, September 17, 46–69.

Shaftel, Fannie R., and George Shaftel. 1967, 1982. *Role Playing in the Curriculum.* Englewood Cliffs, NJ: Prentice Hall.

Shapiro, Bonnie. 1994. *What Children Bring to Light.* New York: Teachers College Press.

Simon, Sidney B. 1973. *Values Clarification: A Handbook of Practical Strategies for Teachers and Students.* New York: Dodd Mead.

Snygg, Donald. 1966. "A Cognitive Field Theory of Learning." In *Learning and Mental Health in the School*, edited by Walter B. Watjean. Washington, DC: Association for Supervision and Curriculum Development.

Wassermann, Selma. 1962. *A Study of the Thinking Related Behaviors of Grade Six Children in the Presence of Selected Materials and Techniques.* Doctoral dissertation, New York University.

———. 1989. "Learning to Value Error." *Childhood Education* 65, no. 4.

———. 2009. *Teaching for Thinking Today: Theory, Strategies and Activities for the K–8 Classroom.* New York: Teachers College Press.

———. 2000. *Serious Players in the Primary Classroom: Empowering Children Through Active Learning Experiences.* New York: Teachers College Press.

———. 2017a. *The Art of Interactive Teaching: Listening, Responding, Questioning.* New York: Routledge.

———. 2017b. "Changing Course: Re-Thinking Education Course Design." *Childhood Education* 93, no. 4: 346–355.

Wassermann, Selma, and George Ivany. 1996. *The New Teaching Elementary Science: Who's Afraid of Spiders?* New York: Teachers College Press.

Wineberg, Sam, and Sarah McGrew. 2016. "Why Students Can't Google Their Way to Truth." *Education Week*, November 1.

Woocher, Fredric D. 1977. "Did Your Eyes Deceive You? Expert Psychological Testimony on the Unreliability of Eyewitness Identification." *Stanford Law Review* 29, no. 5: 969–1030.

Index

About the Author

Selma Wassermann is professor emerita in the Faculty of Education at Simon Fraser University, Vancouver, Canada. Her books include *The Art of Interactive Teaching* (2017); *Teaching for Thinking Today: Theory, Strategies and Activities for the K–8 Classroom* (2009); *This Teaching Life* (2004); *Serious Players in the Primary Classroom* (1990); *The New Teaching Elementary Science* (1988); and *The Long Distance Grandmother* (1988).

www.ingramcontent.com/pod-product-compliance
Lightning Source LLC
Chambersburg PA
CBHW020238290326

41929CB00044B/314